United States
Department of
Agriculture

Forest Service

Pacific Northwest
Research Station

General Technical
Report
PNW-GTR-708
May 2007

The Utility of Strategic Surveys for Rare and Little-Known Species Under the Northwest Forest Plan

Deanna H. Olson, Kelli J. Van Norman, and Robert D. Huff

Authors

Deanna H. Olson is a research ecologist, U.S. Department of Agriculture, Forest Service, Pacific Northwest Research Station, Forestry Sciences Laboratory, 3200 SW Jefferson Way, Corvallis, OR 97330; **Kelli J. Van Norman** is an inventory coordinator and **Robert D. Huff** is a conservation planning coordinator, U.S. Department of the Interior, Bureau of Land Management, Oregon State Office, Interagency Special Status/Sensitive Species Program, 333 SW 1st Avenue, Portland, OR 97208.

Cover art: drawing by Phil Rickus.

Abstract

Olson, Deanna H.; Van Norman, Kelli J.; Huff, Robert D. 2007. The utility of strategic surveys for rare and little-known species under the Northwest Forest Plan. Gen. Tech. Rep. PNW-GTR-708. Portland, OR: U.S. Department of Agriculture, Forest Service, Pacific Northwest Research Station. 48 p.

Management of over 400 rare species thought to be associated with late-successional and old-growth forest conditions on U.S. federal lands within the range of the northern spotted owl (*Strix occidentalis caurina*) included a four-pronged "survey-and-manage" approach in 1994–2004 and 2006–2007, which included predisturbance surveys, strategic surveys, management of known sites to address species' persistence, and adaptive management via an annual species review to improve management approaches. Although the objective of predisturbance surveys was to detect species in areas proposed for land management activities, strategic surveys were intended to fill critical information gaps in species knowledge. Many rare taxa in this program were little known, and basic knowledge of abundance and distribution patterns, species-habitat relationships, or species responses to disturbances were not well understood. To advance the adaptive management of this type of program, we compiled these strategic survey projects and evaluated their relative effectiveness by project types (including known site surveys, purposive surveys, probability surveys, historical data and literature synthesis, modeling, research, and genetics) and 10 taxa (fungi, lichens, bryophytes, vascular plants, arthropods, mollusks, amphibians, red tree voles [*Phenacomys longicaudus*], great gray owl [*Strix nebulosa*], and bats). We tallied 96 projects initiated in this timeframe, with almost $5 million spent for their implementation. From 63 projects, 123 products, (e.g. publications and reports) were compiled and are now available in a regional archive. Although all project types significantly contributed to advancing our understanding of rare species, numerous lessons learned from this effort will be important considerations for future conservation programs.

Keywords: Rare species, adaptive management, inventory, conservation.

Introduction

Biodiversity conservation approaches target both species and habitats (e.g., Lindenmayer and Franklin 2002, Meffe and Carroll 1997, Miller et al. 1995, Noss et al. 1997). Rare species are often the focus of conservation efforts, which can target the species themselves, or surrogate species associated with them, and their habitats. For example, the U.S. Endangered Species Act (ESA) takes a species-by-species approach, yet focuses conservation efforts on protecting or restoring habitats that also serve larger assemblages and ecological processes (Noss et al. 1997). As landscapes or ecosystems are managed for multiple resources, including biodiversity, the list of rare species burgeons. In particular, forests are one of the most species-diverse systems, where an estimated two-thirds of all terrestrial species occur worldwide (World Commission on Forests and Sustainable Development 1999). Surrogate species and habitat management designs can serve as "umbrellas" for larger species communities, including the rare taxa with similar ecologies. However, this coarse-filter approach fails when rare taxa do not have a good spatial correspondence with surrogate species or habitat protections.

Forests are one of the most species-diverse systems, where an estimated two-thirds of all terrestrial species occur worldwide.

This issue was recognized during the development of the U.S. Northwest Forest Plan, which sought to preserve socioeconomic and ecological commodities in the range of the northern spotted owl (*Strix occidentalis caurina*) in western Oregon and Washington and northwestern California (FEMAT 1993; USDA and USDI 1994a, 1994b). An overarching goal of the plan was to address the ESA listing of the owl by a habitat management plan focusing on the 23.7 million acres of federal forest land within its range. The owl is a late-successional and old-growth (LSOG) forest associate, and species assessments during plan development found most LSOG associates in other taxonomic groups would likely be protected by the plan's various habitat provisions (FEMAT 1993). However, there was concern for persistence of over 400 rare or little known species that did not appear to be well protected by reserves or habitat mitigations designed at site-to-ecosystem scales, or for which there was uncertainty regarding these issues. These taxa included fungi, lichens, bryophytes, vascular plants, arthropods, mollusks, amphibians, red tree voles (*Phenacomys longicaudus*), and great gray owls (*Strix nebulosa*). A multipronged "survey-and-manage" program was implemented to address the conservation of these taxa (Molina et al. 2006; USDA and USDI 1994b, 2000, 2001). These prongs included (1) predisturbance surveys, where areas proposed for land management activities that could significantly negatively affect the species are surveyed to detect those present; (2) strategic surveys, designed to gain additional or sometimes basic knowledge about the species; (3) management of known sites to help provide a reasonable assurance of species persistence; and (4) adaptive management via an annual species review process. Although the survey-and-manage program ended in 2004 (USDA and USDI 2004a, 2004b) and at this writing was only recently reinstated in 2006, its approaches warrant evaluation for program adaptive management as well as consideration for application to any similar conservation efforts that attempt to balance natural resource protection with commodity production.

Accrual of new knowledge of species through strategic surveys was intended in part to lead to adaptive management in the survey-and-manage program.

In particular, strategic surveys were an important component of this rare species conservation approach because most "survey-and-manage" taxa were little known. Critical information gaps included basic knowledge of their ecology, including abundance and distribution patterns, micro- and macro-habitat associations, life history, and response to disturbances. Accrual of new knowledge of species through strategic surveys was intended in part to lead to adaptive management in the survey-and-manage program by refinement of predisturbance survey protocols and site management recommendations. This new information also was included in annual reassessments of the conservation status of each survey-and-manage species. This process of continuous collection and evaluation of new information that is subsequently incorporated into management direction is known as adaptive management by federal agencies. This annual species review allowed for removal of species from the program that were determined to be of lesser priority for conservation action or if new information showed the species no longer met criteria for inclusion (Molina et al. 2003, Rittenhouse 2003). These inclusion criteria included the species being rare or uncommon, having a close association with LSOG forest conditions, and species persistence not being provided by federal reserves or other standards and guidelines of the Northwest Forest Plan (e.g., USDA and USDI 2001, 2004c). For example, through strategic surveys it was documented that some species had a more widespread distribution or broader habitat use than was previously recognized. This could inform a management decision that the species did not need the survey-and-manage mitigation to persist on federal lands in the range of the northern spotted owl.

The framework for strategic surveys developed significantly during the course of the survey-and-manage program from 1994 to 2004. Initially, strategic surveys were termed "extensive surveys" and "general regional surveys" and were instituted primarily for the least-known species such as many fungi, lichens, bryophytes, and arthropods (USDA and USDI 1994a, 1994b). In the early years, there was an emphasis on conducting predisturbance surveys because this was specified as a requirement for some species in the record of decision (USDA and USDI 1994a, 1994b), and little financial support was allocated to extensive or general regional surveys. In 2001, this broad survey concept to gather new species information was revisited and applied to all taxa in the program (USDA and USDI 2000, 2001), with a concurrent name change to "strategic surveys." A major underpinning of the strategic surveys was the ability to ask specific questions about the most important information needed per species, and for the species of greatest management concern, so that the best survey and management approach could be developed.

Project Types

Several specific strategic survey approaches or project types were pursued to meet the information needs of the various taxa (Molina et al. 2003; Rittenhouse 2002, 2003). Each project type is described further below. The choice of project type was driven by the level of information and question that needed to be addressed per taxon. For example, if there were few known site data and little known about a taxon (e.g., some lichens, bryophytes, mollusks, and fungi), the priority was to gain some knowledge of its general biology and ecology, especially distribution and habitat associations. Association with late-successional or old-growth forest conditions was a criterion for inclusion in the survey-and-manage program; hence knowing whether or not a taxon had this habitat association was a particular need. Also, another criterion for inclusion as a survey-and-manage species was that the reserve system and other provisions of the federal Northwest Forest Plan did not provide for their persistence; hence, distribution of the organisms relative to land use allocations was another specific information need. Basic information needs about distribution and habitat could lead to the project types of known-site surveys, purposive surveys, probability sampling, and habitat modeling. For taxa with more data on known site locations but little biology and ecology knowledge, statistical modeling could be used to develop predictions about habitat associations (e.g., some mollusks and amphibians). Modeling simulations could be used for those species with more information about their ecology but few known sites. With both ecological knowledge and known-site data available, population and habitat modeling could be developed and validated (e.g., some amphibians). A mix of approaches could be applied to a taxon to address different information needs (e.g., by region), or to opportunistically gain from the interests of different principal investigators proposing projects.

Several specific strategic survey approaches or project types were pursued to meet the information needs of the various taxa.

Known-site surveys—

Surveys of known sites of rare species served two primary purposes: to confirm the continued existence of the species at those sites, and to collect new habitat or population data for further analyses of habitat associations, life history, and population structure (Molina et al. 2003; Rittenhouse 2002, 2003). Some original site records of survey-and-manage species were several decades old. With timber harvest, fire, or other disturbances occurring on the landscape in the interim, there was some skepticism whether species were extant at those sites. For species with very few site records, revisits to those sites to collect additional habitat data were an effective means of improving understanding of their habitat associations. Habitat data collected in this way could be included later in habitat modeling approaches (see below, Rittenhouse 2002, 2003). Application of a standard survey protocol was important for these site revisits in order to later merge data across survey crews or independent efforts into meta-analyses; use of such a protocol also would enhance the effectiveness of later monitoring of these sites (e.g., Molina et al. 2003).

Purposive surveys—
The perceived rarity of some survey-and-manage species likely stems from little past effort to investigate their distributions and habitat associations. If some understanding of habitat and potential distribution existed, the value of intuitive searches by species experts could greatly enhance our knowledge base for such taxa. Purposive surveys were conceived as intuitive or opportunistic searches by experts, with the primary objective of increasing the number of known sites for a species (Molina et al. 2003; Rittenhouse 2002, 2003). This approach could alleviate a concern for species persistence if many new species locations were detected, and could expand our understanding of distribution or habitat use if the organism were to be found in new areas where it had not been reported previously. Also, by providing additional known sites, followup surveys as mentioned above could be completed to meet known-site survey objectives.

Probability sampling—
Probability sampling approaches allow for inference to the broader sampled landscape (Molina et al. 2003). Results of this sampling approach can be an important contributor to species rarity decisions, such as those recommendations for inclusion in the survey-and-manage provision owing to few detection estimates, as well as recommendations for de-listing from the provision when more frequent detection estimates were made, particularly in reserves. Probability sampling designs were developed to address a variety of specific questions about population abundance and distribution, habitat associations, and population trends, for example. Secondarily, such approaches could help studies meet criteria for statistical analyses. A landscape-scale, multiple species survey effort to estimate species occurrences across the Northwest Forest Plan area was launched in 2000 ("random grid" design, Rittenhouse 2002). Through this effort, surveys were conducted for almost 400 rare or little-known species on federal forest lands in the range of the Northwest Forest Plan at existing Forest Inventory and Analysis (FIA) grid points

and Current Vegetation Survey (CVS) points. Sample points were randomly selected within stand-age and land-use strata. Species detections at these points were intended to be incorporated into species occurrence estimators and habitat association models across these lands.

Modeling—

Model-based approaches addressed several species-habitat related questions (Molina et al. 2003, Rittenhouse 2002). Models could be developed to map potential or suitable habitats across the forest landscape, to statistically describe species-associations with those mapped habitat elements, and then spatially portray estimated species occurrences across that same landscape. Models also could be used to forecast species rarity based on existing knowledge, assess risk or persistence concerns, and project species responses to conservation practices. Finally, microhabitat models could identify those specific elements (e.g., coarse woody debris, stream proximity, plant species association) that determine species presence on a site. This information could help refine survey methods to target these features and also aid development of management recommendations for protecting or restoring the most important habitat elements to provide for species persistence.

Research—

Research approaches (Molina et al. 2003, Rittenhouse 2003) could be used to address additional information needs to advance rare species conservation. For example, responses of species to disturbances such as fire or timber harvest, or protections such as reserve islands, could be addressed by research studies using retrospective or before-after-control designs. Survey protocols are not well tested for many taxa, so research could assess efficacy of different approaches. Also, our understanding of rare species' life history or population structures are usually limited and could be augmented by studies of these attributes (see Species-Specific Surveys; Rittenhouse 2002, 2003). In particular, population structure can now be easily understood with application of recently developed genetics techniques. Genetics could be applied to some of the taxa groups in our pool to help define species, as well as population boundaries.

Strategic Survey Implementation

Selection and implementation of any project type depends heavily on the taxon, habitat, specific information need, and objective of the effort (Olson and Leonard 1997). Priorities of information needs were key factors in determining which projects and approaches were chosen for strategic survey implementation (Rittenhouse 2003). High-priority projects included consideration of biological (e.g., persistence),

The objective of our study is to further develop a tracking system for projects, evaluate the approaches used, and summarize lessons learned from the survey-and-manage strategic surveys. We provide the first adaptive management feedback loop for this novel strategic survey concept, and our findings will likely be of use beyond our region, for development of rare species programs globally.

managerial (e.g., cost of management, tradeoffs with other resources), and operational (e.g., specified timelines needed to be met, USDA and USDI 2001) factors (Rittenhouse 2003, USDA and USDI 2004c). Molina et al. (2003) cited several other considerations for selection of strategic survey approaches: efficiency, cost, scientific credibility, and legal defensibility. One particular survey type may be more efficient or cost-effective than the others at addressing the information need given the species, existing knowledge base, or personnel available to conduct the work. Scientific credibility depends on the standard use of protocols and peer-reviewed designs, analyses, and reports when they are relevant, in order to reduce bias and result in findings accepted by both scientists and managers; this will lead to legally defensible decisions (e.g., regarding rarity or persistence) by managers.

The Strategic Survey Implementation Guide (SSIG) (Rittenhouse 2002, 2003) described information needs per species, and specified how strategic surveys were applied to address these knowledge gaps. In 2000-2004, many of these projects were funded and implemented (USDA and USDI 2004c). In 2003, the SSIG briefly summarized project findings (Rittenhouse 2003). A system to adequately track these projects across years and evaluate approaches was nearly developed in 2004 when the survey-and-manage program was eliminated (USDA and USDI 2004a, 2004b).

The objective of our study is to further develop a tracking system for projects, evaluate the approaches used, and summarize lessons learned from the survey-and-manage strategic surveys. We provide recommendations to apply these lessons learned to survey-and-manage or other rare species conservation efforts such as the Interagency Special-Status and Sensitive Species Program of the USDI Bureau of Land Management, Oregon and Washington, and USDA Forest Service, Pacific Northwest Region. Strategic survey implementation was expected to change with time as information needs were identified and prioritized annually (USDA and USDI 2001). Molina et al. (2003) envisioned an evolution of strategic survey approaches as knowledge accrued. They thought the need for general species ecological information would decrease with time, and be replaced with more specific species management information and model-based approaches. We provide the first adaptive management feedback loop for this novel strategic survey concept, and our findings will likely be of use beyond our region, for development of rare species programs globally.

Our approach includes four steps. First, we developed a master list of strategic survey projects, including brief information regarding their principal investigators, objectives, direct costs, progress, and key findings. We examined this implementation data across project types (e.g., known-site survey, purposive survey, probability survey, modeling, research) and taxa. Our list included all projects except the random multiple-species survey effort (random grid design); a separate summary has been initiated for that project. Second, we evaluated the projects. Our evaluations were a qualitative panel assessment of project effectiveness to address their objectives, species conservation needs, and project cost efficiency relative to results obtained. We summarized these evaluations by each project type and taxon. Third, we synthesized lessons learned from this effort and opportunities for future work that could fold into the future evolution of similar species conservation efforts. Lastly, we compiled products resulting from these survey efforts in order to develop an information archive for scientists and managers working with these taxa.

Methods

We compiled strategic survey projects by querying several sources in the summer of 2004. First, we reviewed records of projects in the SSIG (Rittenhouse 2002, 2003), and reports and files kept by the survey-and-manage strategic survey coordinator. However, project compilation was not straightforward because the survey-and-manage program had been eliminated before compilation began. As a result, personnel changes had removed knowledgeable persons (e.g., the strategic survey coordinator), and hardcopy or electronic files were not found or did not appear to be complete. Second, we examined annual budget spreadsheets for the survey-and-manage program where either projects or individuals were listed under one of several broader categories. Several individuals were contacted to find out if they had conducted any project that could fall under the category of strategic surveys. Third, we asked taxa leads and experts funded by the survey-and-manage program if they knew of any additional surveys or research. We compiled projects that were directly funded by the strategic survey budget, and also projects that appeared to meet strategic survey information needs but were only indirectly funded through survey-and-manage program operations. For example, some taxa leads funded by the program conducted purposive surveys, revisits to known sites, or research.

We developed a summary form to document each project (app. 1). Forms included information about the project leads, funding received, objectives, critical information gaps addressed, methods, key findings, products, effectiveness, and completion date. These forms were drafted, internally reviewed by program personnel, and revised before use. Forms were sent to project leads, or if leads were not available, to knowledgeable persons associated with the project or taxa. We completed some forms when project leads were unavailable but final reports or publications were available with the relevant project information.

Project evaluations were conducted by a panel in the summer of 2005. Evaluations focused on giving a numerical ranking of the effectiveness of a project's (1) *methods* at addressing the stated objective; (2) implementation at addressing the *conservation* need; and (3) *cost,* in terms of funding provided by the survey-and-manage program, to answer conservation questions.

Information from summary forms was compiled. Funding compiled from the project leads' numbers on summary forms were totaled by project type and taxon. Hence, our results of strategic survey costs were not derived from internal program records, and may differ from other expense compilations relying on other sources. Survey objectives were summarized across projects. Projects that were listed in the SSIG of 2002 and 2003 were tallied by project type and taxon. Strategic survey funding of those not in the guide was summed. Products were listed and attempts were made to find hardcopies of publications or reports. Incomplete projects were highlighted for possible followup.

Project evaluations were conducted by a panel in the summer of 2005. Evaluations focused on giving a numerical ranking of the effectiveness of a project's (1) **methods** at addressing the stated objective; (2) implementation at addressing the **conservation** need; and (3) **cost**, in terms of funding provided by the survey-and-manage program, to answer conservation questions. A 0 to 10 ranking scale was used, with 0 indicating lack of effectiveness and 10 indicating most effective. A score of 5 was generally understood to be "average," and ranks were relative among projects. We also compiled notes regarding accountability issues that may have explained incomplete projects, lessons learned from the project or project implementation, and opportunities for future work. The project evaluation form was drafted, reviewed internally by agency personnel working with the agency sensitive and special status species programs, and revised before use (app. 2). We then conducted a preliminary evaluation of several projects to ensure our form questions were clear and resulted in useful information.

Although we initially planned to have our evaluation panel include field unit biologists and managers who were not closely associated with the survey-and-manage program to reduce bias in our evaluations, we found that the project summary forms we evaluated in this preliminary assessment were extremely brief and required either additional knowledge or considerable explanation for their interpretation. We felt personnel who had been previously associated with survey-and-manage would be most effective at conducting evaluations. Time to conduct evaluations figured into our perception of panel effectiveness; when personnel with knowledge of a project were available, the project could be assessed in about 5 to 20 minutes, whereas it could take twice this time and a mediator to explain additional details of projects when less experienced personnel were used. Hence, four persons with survey-and-manage experience were chosen as panel members. The survey-and-manage roles of these four persons were broad, some had changed over time, and had included being a taxa expert, the acting program manager, the acting strategic survey coordinator, the annual species review coordinator, and the database manager. We acknowledge that such a team of persons tightly linked to the program may bias evaluations; however, we opted for potential bias as a tradeoff to task efficiency, in particular relative to panel logistics and time constraints.

Our evaluations were conducted over a 4-day period with projects clustered by type. For example, we evaluated all known site surveys first. We used a modified Delphi method for the evaluations. The panel convened, panelists each read the summary form for a project, and each panelist completed an evaluation form for the project. When all panelists had completed their evaluations, each revealed their rankings. Panelists then discussed their knowledge of the project and rationale for their rankings; in particular, panelists with both high and low scores for effectiveness questions revealed why they had up- or down-graded projects. Finally, panelists were provided the opportunity to recast their rating given the new information provided by others. We did not attempt to reach consensus for ranked or other questions, but we recorded the variety of scores and opinions given. In some cases, panelists did not have sufficient information to score a project and a question mark was given for an element on the form. Ranked scores were averaged, with question marks omitted from the averaging. We listed "action items" for incomplete projects, projects which we felt required broader dissemination, or projects with opportunities for additional work.

Methods, conservation, and cost-effectiveness evaluations were summarized per project type and per taxon. Average, maximum, and minimum effectiveness scores were examined for ranked questions. When a project addressed more than one taxon, it was compiled and evaluated separately for each taxon. Similarly, in a couple of cases, a project had multiple objectives, which met the criteria for more than one project type; these were compiled and evaluated separately for each project type. Overall project effectiveness was calculated as the sum of the three ranked effectiveness scores. Average project conservation and overall effectiveness scores were examined relative to whether or not a project was identified in the SSIG. Overall effectiveness was categorized and compared to funding levels provided by the strategic survey program; patterns of effectiveness by funding level were examined. Lastly, information was compiled for other questions on the evaluation form including lessons learned, accountability issues, and future work opportunities.

We reviewed 96 projects. At the time of our evaluation, 41 of 96 (43 percent) of projects were not completed, and completion was unknown for two projects.

Results

We reviewed 96 projects and their corresponding summary forms from August 2004 to August 2005. Our total sample size of projects by project type was 98 (two projects had objectives relevant to different project types), and by taxa was 120 (15 projects addressed multiple taxa, 5 projects addressed "All Taxa" and were compiled separately). At the time of our evaluation, 41 of 96 (43 percent) of projects were not completed, and completion was unknown for two projects. Of the 41 incomplete projects, two had not been begun at all, we thought many may have been either stopped or stalled by the elimination of the survey-and-manage program in 2004, and some were ongoing.

Project objectives were quite variable. Many projects gathered information about habitat attributes at known sites or modeled species-habitat associations or did both. Historical data were compiled, including literature citations and known-site information. Genetics studies identified discrete populations that may warrant discrete conservation measures. Effects of forest management activities on taxa were examined in several instances (e.g., arthropods, lichens). Species ranges were explored, and in some cases rarity was confirmed.

Funding compiled from summary forms for these strategic survey projects reached almost $5 million dollars (table 1), excluding the random multiple-species survey. If funding amounts were not always clear from our records in 2004, estimates were made by principal investigators or survey-and-manage personnel; some project funding may have been over- or underestimated owing to sparse records. Of the 120 projects by taxa, 89 appeared to be funded directly by the survey-and-manage program. As taxa groups, amphibians and lichens received the greatest amount of funding, with bats and great gray owls receiving the least funding. Red tree vole was the most-funded taxon, receiving a half million dollars for 10 projects. On a per-species basis, five amphibians and the great gray owl received over $90,000 per species in project funding. With 189 fungi species identified in the survey-and-manage program (table 1), their funding allocation on a per-species basis was smallest, at $2,350 per species.

More projects were conducted with amphibians (n = 27) and bryophytes (n = 21) than other taxa groups (table 1). However, 13 of the 27 (48 percent) amphibian projects and 6 of the 21 (28.5 percent) bryophyte projects were not directly funded by the strategic survey program (table 1). Not including unfunded projects, the count of projects by taxa ranged from 1 for bats to 15 for bryophytes, and averaged 8 per taxon group.

Among taxa, different project types were implemented (fig. 1). The most common project types were modeling (n = 30), purposive surveys (n = 17), research (n = 17), and probability sampling (n = 13). Modeling was most frequently applied to amphibians (n = 12 projects), mollusks (n = 5), and lichens (n = 5). For species with little prior information about them, purposive surveys were frequently used to gain basic knowledge: bryophytes (n = 11 projects) and fungi (n = 3). Similarly, for species with little prior habitat information, known-site surveys were used with

Funding compiled from summary forms for these strategic survey projects reached almost $5 million dollars.

Table 1—Tally of strategic survey projects and related studies and their cost by taxa, and sum of taxa in the survey-and-manage program in 2001

Taxon	Number of projects		Total cost	Average cost per funded project	Number of taxa
	Funded	**Unfunded**			
			Thousand dollars		
All taxa	4	1	473	118	—
Amphibians	14	13	836	60	5
Arthropods	7	0	626	89	4 assemblages
Bats	1	0	148	148	—
Bryophytes	15	6	325	22	17
Fungi	11	4	445	40	209
Great gray owl	2	0	185	92	1
Lichens	12	3	780	65	51
Mollusks	7	4	381	54	46
Red tree vole	10	0	502	50	1
Vascular plants	6	0	292	49	12
Total	89	31	4,993	56	346

— = not applicable.

[a] Of the 96 projects conducted, some addressed more than one taxon, and these were counted for each taxon here (hence, no. projects = 120), whereas their costs were divided equally among taxa in the project (funding was not double counted). "Funded" projects were allocated monies from the survey-and-manage program under the auspices of strategic surveys. "Unfunded" projects may have been funded by other means but were conducted on survey-and-manage species and had objectives similar to other strategic survey projects.
Source: USDA and USDI 2001.

bryophytes (n = 5 projects) and fungi, lichens, and vascular plants (n = 3, each); and historical data compilations (n = 5 projects) were conducted on bryophytes, lichens, red tree voles, and arthropods. One or two research projects per taxon were conducted for fungi, great gray owl, lichens, mollusks, and vascular plants; and five research projects were conducted with amphibians and five with arthropods. Probability sampling was implemented to make population inferences with some species: amphibians and red tree vole (n = 4 projects each), lichens and fungi (n = 2, each) and bats (n = 1). Five to six different project types were used with amphibians, fungi, lichens, and red tree voles; and four different types were used with bryophytes, mollusks, and vascular plants. Three modeling projects and two program development projects were applicable to all taxa. "Program development" was a project type submitted by two principal investigators who had been funded to assist in the design of the strategic survey program. Their work related to how the strategic survey program could be developed, including identification of project types and how information needs per taxon could be compiled and evaluated.

Affiliations of principal investigators of strategic survey projects included federal agency personnel, university cooperators, and independent contractors

Affiliations of principal investigators of strategic survey projects included federal agency personnel, university cooperators, and independent contractors.

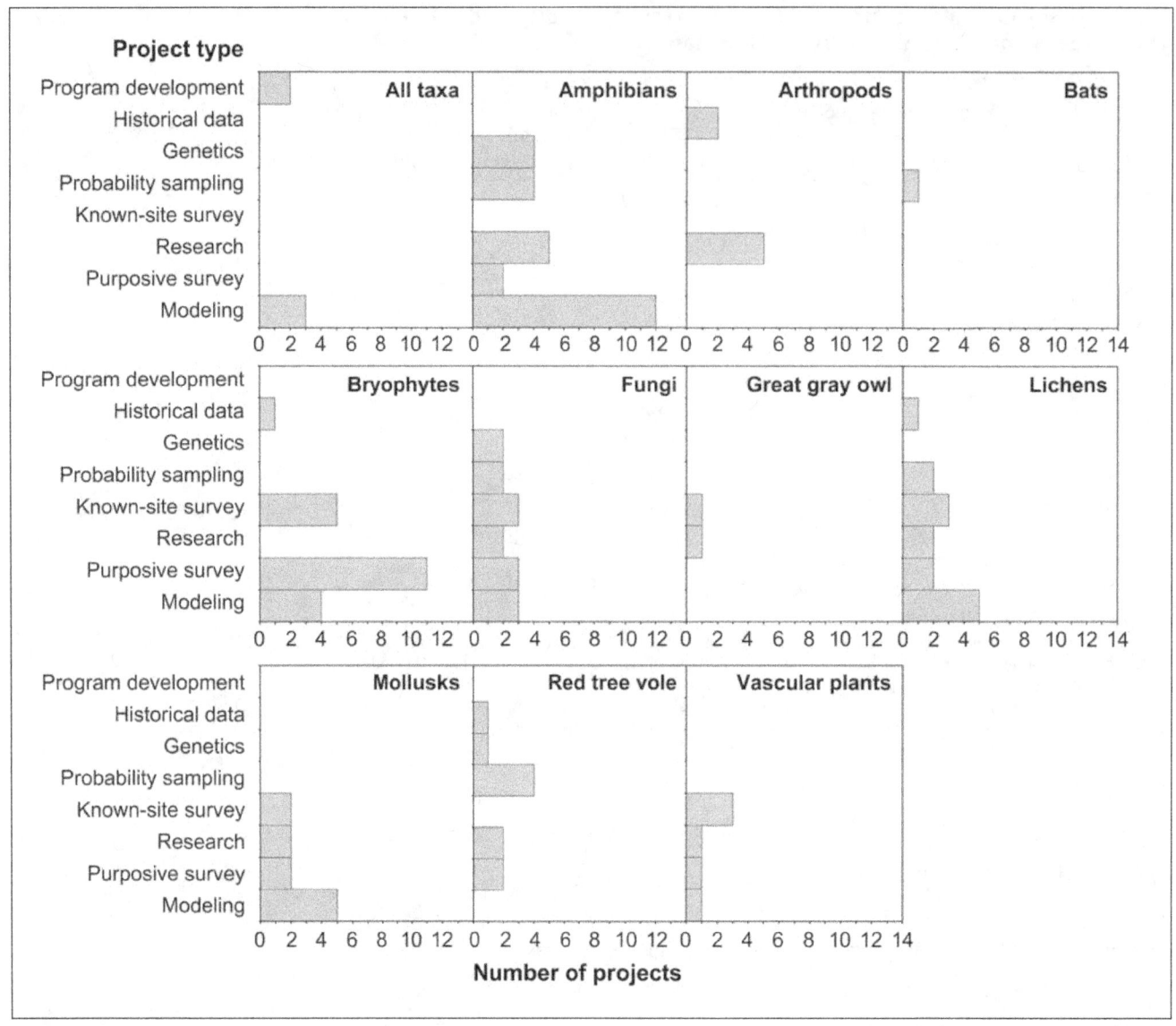

Figure 1—Number of strategic survey projects conducted by project type per taxon.

(table 2). Most investigators were affiliated with the USDA Forest Service, being employed by the Pacific Northwest Research Station (PNW, mainly at the Forestry Sciences Laboratory, Corvallis, OR), the Pacific Southwest Research Station (PSW, Redwood Sciences Laboratory, Arcata, CA), or the National Forest System (NFS). For both the USDI Bureau of Land Management (BLM) and the USDA Forest Service National Forest System, we did not distinguish between those working at regional, state, or field unit offices. Investigators from both Forest Service Pacific Southwest and Pacific Northwest Regions were noted, however. For projects that were a mix of affiliations, if a single investigator or affiliation took primary responsibility for the work, they alone were included in our compilation here. For example,

Table 2—Affiliations of strategic survey project principal investigators by project type and taxonomic group[a]

	Affiliation								
	University	Contract	USGS	BLM	NFS	PSW	PNW	USFWS	Mix
Project type:									
Genetics	4	1	1	0	0	0	0	0	0
Historical data compilation	1	1	0	0	1	0	1	0	0
Known-site surveys	0	1	0	1	4	0	1	0	1
Modeling	3	0	2	0	10	6	6	1	0
Probability sampling	0	1	0	1	3	1	7	0	0
Program development	0	0	1	0	1	0	0	0	0
Purposive survey	0	9	0	0	4	0	1	1	0
Research	2	0	0	0	3	1	10	0	0
Taxonomic group:									
Amphibians	6	1	1	0	2	5	12	0	0
Arthropods	2	1	0	0	0	0	4	0	0
Bats	0	0	0	0	0	1	0	0	0
Bryophytes	1	6	0	0	10	1	1	1	1
Fungi	0	4	0	0	3	0	4	0	1
Great gray owl	0	0	0	1	1	0	0	0	0
Lichens	1	1	1	0	10	1	0	0	1
Mollusks	1	3	1	0	2	2	1	0	1
Red tree vole	1	0	1	1	2	0	4	0	0
Vascular plants	1	1	0	0	0	0	0	0	1
Other	0	0	0	0	0	0	1	0	0
All	0	0	0	0	2	0	0	1	0

[a] University = university collaborators; contract = independent contractors; USGS = U.S. Geological Survey; BLM = U.S. Bureau of Land Management; NFS = U.S. Forest Service, National Forest System; PSW = U.S. Forest Service, Pacific Southwest Research Station; PNW = U.S. Forest Service, Pacific Northwest Research Station; USFWS = U.S. Fish and Wildlife Service; mix = mixture of affiliations.

if a PNW collaborator working with a university student on a project was the responsible party for the work, their PNW affiliation was counted in our tally.

Patterns of affiliation by project type and taxa were apparent (table 2). University collaborators conducted primarily genetics, modeling, and research studies. Independent contractors were hired for many purposive surveys. Modeling was conducted by the NFS, PNW, and PSW, primarily. Probability sampling and research projects were dominated by investigators from NFS and PNW. By taxa, investigator affiliation patterns included amphibian projects conducted by university cooperators, PNW, and PSW; bryophyte projects conducted by independent contractors and NFS; fungi projects conducted by independent contractors, NFS, and PNW; lichen projects conducted by NFS; and PNW researchers contributing to red tree vole and arthropod studies.

Most projects were identified, at least in a general sense, in the SSIG of 2002 or 2003 (Rittenhouse 2002, 2003). By project type, 70 percent of projects were identified in the guide, and 76 percent of these were funded directly by the strategic survey program. Of those **not** referenced in the guide, the most frequent project types were research (n = 9), genetics (n = 5), purposive surveys, and modeling (n = 4, each). By project type, overall, 64 percent of those **not** named in the guide were funded by the strategic survey program. Tallying by taxa group, 73 percent of projects were identified in the guide, with 79 percent of them being funded by the program. Of those not found in the guide, most frequent projects by taxa were amphibian (n = 9), bryophyte (n = 6), fungi, and all taxa (n = 4, each), and overall, with 64 percent of these being program funded. The sum of direct funding from the strategic survey program toward projects not referenced in the guide was estimated at $770,000; this was about 15 percent of the total funding allocation.

Evaluations of Summary Forms

Project effectiveness—

Ranking of effectiveness was conducted by a four-person panel on a 10-point scale (10 = highest effectiveness, 5 = "average") for three aspects of projects: **methods**, **conservation**, and **cost**. **Methods** effectiveness addressed how well a project's method was conceptually able to meet the project objectives. Although a proposal may have had an effective design a priori, we ranked the implementation of the project's method here if that information differed from the proposed methods. For example, if a project proposed to use a random site selection for surveys, but ended up with a nonrandom and biased design, its ranking was likely lowered because of implementation issues. A lower score for methods effectiveness indicated a flawed design for the stated objectives. These scores ranged from 0 to 9.5 across projects, and overall were the highest scores of the three aspects. Average methods effectiveness across project types was 7.46, and across taxa was 7.49 (exclusive of bats, which were not survey-and-manage, and which had only one project with a score of 3.25; with this score added, the mean taxa score was 7.10).

Conservation effectiveness addressed how well a project's results actually met information needs by the survey-and-manage program, for example to improve surveys, to improve management approaches, or to fill critical information needs for taxa. A high score in this category indicated the conservation of a taxon was advanced by the findings of the project. Conservation effectiveness of projects ranged from 0 to 9.25, averaged 6.19 for project types and 6.18 for taxa (bats were excluded because no score was given for this aspect).

Cost effectiveness addressed the cost of a project, and how well the funding level matched information needs given the scope of the work conducted. A highly

Methods **effectiveness addressed how well a project's method was conceptually able to meet the project objectives.** *Conservation* **effectiveness addressed how well a project's results actually met information needs by the survey-and-manage program, for example to improve surveys, to improve management approaches, or to fill critical information needs for taxa.**

ranked score in cost effectiveness indicated a lot of useful information was collected for relatively little or a reasonable amount of funding. Cost effectiveness scores ranged from 0 to 9.25 among projects, with a mean score of 6.29 by project type and a mean score of 5.99 by taxa (excluding the one bat project; with it included, the mean by taxa score was 5.71).

By project type (fig. 2a), mean methods effectiveness was highest for genetics and historic data compilation (> 8.0) and lowest for known-site surveys and purposive surveys (< 6.5). Historical data compilation received the highest score for conservation effectiveness (7.46), followed by probability sampling (6.95), and genetics (6.62). Known-site surveys were ranked lower for conservation effectiveness (4.75). Historical data compilation also received the highest score for cost effectiveness (7.75). Research received the lowest cost effectiveness score (5.27).

By taxa (fig. 2b), methods effectiveness scores averaged 6.27 to 8.32 (excluding bats, 3.25 for one project). Arthropods and amphibians received the highest methods rankings, whereas lichens and bryophytes received the lowest. For both conservation and cost effectiveness, great gray owl, arthropods, and amphibians were ranked high. Lower scores (< 6.0) for conservation effectiveness were received by the all taxa category, vascular plants, red tree voles, lichens, and bryophytes. Lower cost scores (< 6.0) were given to all taxa, bryophytes, lichens, mollusks, and vascular plants (and bats, 3.0).

By project, summed scores across all three aspects (methods, conservation, and cost effectiveness, sum = 30 maximum) gave an overall ranking of project efficacy. The most effective projects had sums > 27, and included an arthropod project that conducted a literature search synthesizing knowledge of forest arthropods and an amphibian research project advancing risk assessment procedures by use of landscape geographic information system parameters, which could be applied to any taxa. Eight additional projects received summed scores ≥ 24: three amphibian projects, two lichen projects, one fungi research project, a second arthropod literature synthesis, and one project with fungi, bryophytes, and lichens. Least effective projects had summed ranks ranging from 0 to 12: two lichen and one mollusk project for which there was no support for them to have been conducted despite funding allocation (summed ranks of zero), and one bryophyte project, which may have been completed but for which the product had not been submitted (summed rank of 8).

Average conservation and overall effectiveness were computed for projects identified and those not identified in the SSIGs (Rittenhouse 2002, 2003). Conservation effectiveness averaged 6.6 for projects listed as a priority in the SSIGs, and it

Cost effectiveness addressed the cost of a project, and how well the funding level matched information needs given the scope of the work conducted. A highly ranked score in cost effectiveness indicated a lot of useful information was collected for relatively little or a reasonable amount of funding.

By project, summed scores across all three aspects (methods, conservation, and cost effectiveness, sum = 30 maximum) gave an overall ranking of project efficacy.

averaged 5.2 for those not in the SSIG (unranked projects were not included, n = 1 for unranked SSIG projects and n = 3 for unranked non-SSIG). However, four projects received a zero ranking among those not listed in the SSIG, and no zeroes occurred in the SSIG group. A zero ranking meant we had no evidence that the project was actually conducted. Removing the four projects with zeroes from the tally, the average increased to 6.2 for projects not in the SSIGs. Overall effectiveness was the sum of the three rankings (methods, conservation, and cost) and did not include projects lacking one of these rankings (26 percent of SSIG projects lacked a score, 40 percent of non-SSIG projects). Average overall effectiveness for SSIG projects was 20.5, and for non-SSIG projects was 15.8. Again, removing the four projects that did not appear to have been conducted (zero ranks for conservation and cost effectiveness), the average overall effectiveness for non-SSIG projects increased to 20.8.

Overall project effectiveness was also examined relative to the extent of strategic survey funding provided to projects. An interesting pattern occurred where projects funded by more than $30,000 were ranked higher in overall effectiveness, with the majority of these projects receiving summed rankings $\geq$20 (table 3).

Other findings—

Lessons learned per project were key points, both positive and negative, compiled during panel evaluations. We found these spanned advances relative to species biology and ecology, survey methods development, and forest management considerations (app. 3). It is important to note that these "lessons" did not highlight all new information (e.g., species sites, research findings) gained from a project. We also found several project implementation issues, including need for greater project planning, documentation, or accountability (37 of 96 projects [38.5 percent], app. 3). Two types of projects were perceived to be potentially expensive when they were conducted on a per-species basis: molecular genetic probes for species identification and habitat modeling.

A final section of the evaluation forms addressed those topics recommended to be followed up by subsequent federal agency programs. These included project completion or publication (n = 9 projects), incorporation of information into conservation assessments (n = 4), agency acquisition of products (n = 2), and data entry (n = 4). However, consideration of new work dominated recommendations (n = 43), such as collection of new data, habitat analysis, modeling, model validation (n = 25), conducting new syntheses (n = 2), and using sites for monitoring (n = 3).

Table 3—Project cost categories in relation to overall effectiveness ranks (sum of methods, conservation and cost ranks per project, potential range 0–30)[a]

Cost category ($1,000)	Overall effectiveness				
	<10	10–14.9	15–19.9	20–24.9	25–30
<10	1	2	3	2	—
10–29	3	2	7	1	—
30–49	—	—	3	5	2
50–69	—	—	1	8	—
70–89	—	1	—	5	—
90–109	—	—	—	2	—
110–199	—	—	3	10	—
>200	—	—	3	—	—

— Indicates no projects were sorted into that cell.

[a] Costs are funds allocated to the project through the strategic survey program. Projects without direct funding from strategic surveys and projects that were not scored for all three effectiveness measures are not included.

Products

Products from projects included reports, publications, and references of oral or poster presentations given of project findings. We compiled hardcopies of 123 reports and publications from 63 projects during our evaluation (app. 4).

Discussion

The strategic survey program was a component of survey-and-manage instituted to fill critical information gaps regarding rare and little-known species' basic biology, life history, distribution, and abundance patterns. Specifically, strategic surveys targeted those information needs relevant to advancing species' management efficacies on federal lands within the range of the northern spotted owl. Some projects focused on validating whether or not species met survey-and-manage criteria (i.e., being associated with LSOG forest conditions, that reserves did not provide for persistence, and that the taxon was rare). Improved knowledge in these areas could reduce the list of species being managed under the survey-and-manage program, which would have direct managerial repercussions by focusing future efforts on the truly rare and at-risk species, and also could result in the lifting of restrictions on projects, and potential economic ramifications if commodity production was facilitated. Validation that species met the criteria of the survey-and-manage program could focus future resources to more specific aspects of their ecology, to improve species management approaches.

Our compilation and evaluation of strategic surveys and related projects to date has provided significant insight regarding implementation, scope, and effectiveness of the survey-and-manage strategic survey program. Although most projects

We compiled hardcopies of 123 reports and publications from 63 projects during our evaluation.

successfully met their objectives, many were incomplete at the time of our evaluation, and we were not able to find evidence that a few were conducted as planned. Nevertheless, each project has contributed important lessons learned about project and program implementation. Their value is often in the species knowledge gained, the implementation lessons learned, and the opportunities they have opened for pursuit by others.

Project Compilation

Ninety-six distinct projects were compiled in our assessment of strategic surveys and related projects from 1994 to 2004. The SSIG (Rittenhouse 2002, 2003) served as a synthesis of projects being funded by the program. Of those 96 projects we compiled, 70 percent were named in the SSIG. Of those projects we found were funded by the strategic survey program, 15 percent were not reported in the SSIG. Although the guide adequately represented the main projects being pursued, it was not a mechanism to account for all projects being conducted. The 2003 SSIG also contained some project findings. However, again, these were syntheses, and did not fully explain projects and their findings. An additional tracking mechanism would be warranted to fulfill the task of complete accountability of projects, from funding of proposals through project completion and reporting. We found considerable "detective work" was needed to identify some project leads and findings of studies, suggesting that a tracking system would be useful. To this end, we now have a database of projects with summary information (app. 1) and products compiled (app. 4) in an information archive. This will be an important step, considering that over 40 percent of projects were not completed at the time of our synthesis.

Most projects were species- or taxon-specific because information needs differed with taxa and geographic locations (Rittenhouse 2002, 2003), and project methods were often taxon-specific. However, one-fifth of the projects spanned multiple taxa, suggesting that cross-taxonomic efficiencies were being sought. In several projects, taxa included together for projects involving field surveys or modeling were lichens, bryophytes, and fungi. Commonalities among these taxa may include habitat associations, survey approaches, and level of knowledge.

We summarized eight project types overall. During the development of the strategic survey program, five of these eight project types had been identified (known-site surveys, purposive surveys, probability surveys, modeling, and research). Two of the additional three types we recognized in our assessment are subcategories of "research": historical data compilation and genetics. Historical data compilation included literature review and known-site compilation. Although these are relevant

Our compilation and evaluation of strategic surveys and related projects to date has provided significant insight regarding implementation, scope, and effectiveness of the survey-and-manage strategic survey program.

research tasks, this work differs significantly from collection of new information to answer a specific question typical of other research projects. Historical data compilation occurred for many taxa outside the guise of strategic surveys, for example at the beginning of the survey-and-manage program in 1994 and 1995 or as literature was synthesized to write early management recommendations and survey protocols. The projects included here are only the later efforts initiated that were funded by strategic surveys. Genetics studies were broken out from "research" owing to their common question of seeking recognition of species or populations by using molecular laboratory tools, and their frequency (n = 7 genetics projects) relative to all other research projects (n = 17). The last type of project we identified was "Program Development." We received summary forms from a couple of project leads because they were funded to develop strategic survey program procedures. We suspect our summaries of this type of work are underrepresented in our compilation owing to other personnel funded for such work not recognizing or summarizing it as such during our queries for "strategic survey project summaries." However, it does provide insight for program management that procedural development is a critical aspect of program implementation.

All project types were valuable tools to collect new species information. The utility of specific project types depended on the information gap that needed to be addressed, and the prior information available for a taxon. For example, prior to habitat modeling, sufficient species site and habitat data were needed; hence, models could not be developed for the lesser known taxa. There tended to be taxonomic patterns for project types used, and these tracked information needs, site and habitat data, and opportunities owing to personnel expertise or proximity of federal lands to species experts.

The most frequent project types compiled were modeling, purposive surveys, and probability surveys. Modeling and probability surveys have broader inference to a species, habitat, or area, and were likely pursued in order to reveal new information about a species and its habitat. Purposive surveys were initiated to find more species locations, delineate ranges, and collect species' habitat data as the basis for habitat models. However, habitat models developed from purposive survey data are biased and require probability sample data for model testing. Because areas selected to be surveyed by purposive surveys are biased, the results cannot be inferred to a broader area. Another problem with purposive surveys is that often only suspected habitats are searched when the species may occur in other habitat types.

We received summary forms for projects on 10 different taxonomic groups, and some projects appeared conceptually relevant to "All Taxa." Priority taxa for projects appeared to be based on a mixture of management concern, prior information

All project types were valuable tools to collect new species information. The utility of specific project types depended on the information gap that needed to be addressed, and the prior information available for a taxon. The most frequent project types compiled were modeling, purposive surveys, and probability surveys.

We received summary forms for projects on 10 different taxonomic groups, and some projects appeared conceptually relevant to "All Taxa."

about a taxon, personnel, and ability to survey a taxon. Arthropods, bats, and great gray owls were the least-represented taxa among projects, likely because of their reduced emphasis in the survey-and-manage program. Of these three taxa, only arthropods were initially on the survey-and-manage list. In 1994, four arthropod assemblages were identified as survey-and-manage "strategy 4" (i.e., conduct general regional surveys) in the Northwest Forest Plan (USDA and USDI 1994b). Three of these assemblages were of concern in only the "south range": canopy herbivores, coarse wood chewers, and litter and soil dwelling species. The other assemblage was understory and forest gap herbivores. These are all little-known taxa, and primarily literature reviews and management-effects research were initiated to fill knowledge gaps with this taxon. Bat habitat mitigations were a separate provision of the Northwest Forest Plan for matrix lands (USDA and USDI 1994b: C-43-44) and reflected a modified approach of surveys and management of detected sites. The revised survey-and-manage program did not include bats on the species list but refined these mitigations for bats (USDA and USDI 2001: 37-38). Although bats were not within the survey-and-manage program, the program did fund a single probability survey project for this taxon. The great gray owl was a protection buffer species in the original Northwest Forest Plan (USDA and USDI 1994b), and the revised survey-and-manage standards and guidelines formally added this species to the survey-and-manage list (USDA and USDI 2001). Known-site surveys and a research study were funded for these owls. Of the other seven taxa, fewer projects were tallied for vascular plants and mollusks. Priority taxa for implementation of strategic surveys were amphibians, red tree voles, bryophytes, fungi, and lichens. The most projects compiled for a single species were for red tree voles.

Direct funding to 89 strategic survey projects was almost $5 million (table 1). This cost estimate may be low owing to our difficulty in identifying projects that had been conducted, and in determining if survey-and-manage monies may have been indirectly allocated to help pay for some studies (i.e., via salaries covered under other topics in the larger survey-and-manage budget). Funding allocations reflect more overall spending for amphibians, fungi, lichens, and red tree voles. These taxa had direct expenditures from the strategic survey program exceeding $400,000 per taxon. Red tree voles were the single most-funded species ($502,000). These priorities may reflect a focus on projects to advance knowledge of vertebrate species and for taxa with many rare or uncommon species (lichens, fungi). Many lichens and fungi did not require preproject surveys, so strategic surveys were the only mechanism available to gain new information about these little-known taxa.

Two vertebrates, Del Norte salamander (*Plethodon elongatus*) and red tree vole, were entirely (salamander) or partially (voles, some geographic locations) removed from the survey-and-manage program largely as a result of strategic survey findings; for voles this was an outcome of $500,000 in spending decisions, and for salamanders, the cost to the program was about $200,000. Red tree voles reportedly were a huge barrier to timber sales; consequently, removal of them from the program likely facilitated forest management wood production. Similarly, a purposive survey for the bryophyte *Encalypta brevicola* var. *crumiana* determined it was not an old-growth-forest associated species, and it was subsequently removed from survey-and-manage during an annual species review. However, we did not find an explicit rationale documenting that these animals' projects were funded in order for the species to be removed from the list.

Funding averages per project reflect the high cost of projects for taxa that are difficult to study. As a single species, the $185,000 allocated for the two great gray owl projects was similar to funding provided for several amphibian species. If those projects had been completed and survey-and-manage had been retained in 2004, it would have been interesting to see if additional changes in the categorization of these species would have resulted. Some reasons for the discrepancy in project implementation or funding among taxa likely were that the federal agency research community was not well staffed for nonvertebrates, nonvertebrate knowledge gaps were harder to fill because the information gaps are so large by comparison, and some nonvertebrate groups may not have as much of an economic impact and less perceived regulatory attention.

Strategic surveys were a multiagency program of work. Principal investigators belonged to nine affiliation categories.

Strategic surveys were a multiagency program of work. Principal investigators belonged to nine affiliation categories (table 2), seven of which included federal personnel from four agencies: USDI Geological Survey; USDI Bureau of Land Management; USDI Fish and Wildlife Service; and USDA Forest Service. Patterns of investigator affiliation by project type likely reflected the regional expertise available (e.g., established genetics laboratories at universities and ecological modelers at PSW) or efficacies of funding mechanisms to conduct specific work (e.g., purposive surveys conducted by independent contractors). Similarly, taxonomic expertise of investigators by affiliation also was apparent (e.g., PNW expertise in amphibians, arthropods, fungi and red tree voles; NFS expertise in bryophytes and lichens). Implementation of strategic surveys clearly was a complex partnership among numerous independent entities. This led to some important lessons learned, as described below.

Effectiveness

Effectiveness scores were qualitative assessments, and overall showed all project types were fairly successful. Although quantitative comparisons of effectiveness scores among project types or taxa are difficult, interesting patterns can be seen. Of the three aspects of project effectiveness (methods, conservation, and cost), methods scores were highest. This makes sense because, although the design of a project could be well conceived to meet its objectives, conservation and cost scores take into consideration the implementation and findings of the project. Unforeseen logistical constraints may affect implementation, although findings rely upon completion of the complete cycle of a project: design, implementation, data compilation, analyses, and reporting. The fact that many projects were incomplete during our evaluation likely lowered their conservation or cost effectiveness scores. Conservation or cost effectiveness may not have been ranked if progress was uncertain; however, if a project was known to be ongoing or progress reports documented early findings, confidence in project completion was higher and effectiveness scores may have been projected given available information. Also, many projects advanced our knowledge of the biology or site-locations of organisms, but these may have had limited conservation effectiveness if the scope of the new knowledge was limited. Thus although a significant biological or site-specific finding may have developed, these may not have had substantial conservation effectiveness. Some projects collected site and associated habitat data for inclusion in habitat modeling, to be executed via another companion project. In some cases, we could not ensure the data were collected and included in the models, nor did we have evidence to support the development of models. This type of scenario resulted in a lower ranking of conservation and cost effectiveness, with panel notes recorded about project accountability (see below). Lower cost effectiveness scores also may reflect a bias among panelists to expect projects to be more economically implemented, or may reflect more rankings toward a notion of "average" cost effectiveness. It may be difficult to place a monetary value on species information.

Several patterns were apparent by project type and taxa (figs. 2a and 2b). First, it should be noted that the range of scores per category shows many ranks were high. Some categories with a very low score, such as a zero ranking, lowered the mean. Hence a few poorly ranked projects likely shifted averages downward, and patterns may not be truly reflective of the effectiveness of that project category. Nevertheless, patterns should be noted in case their explanation can provide insights to program advancement.

By project type (fig. 2a), genetics had the highest methods effectiveness rank even though it was used by a variety of taxa: amphibians, fungi, and red tree voles.

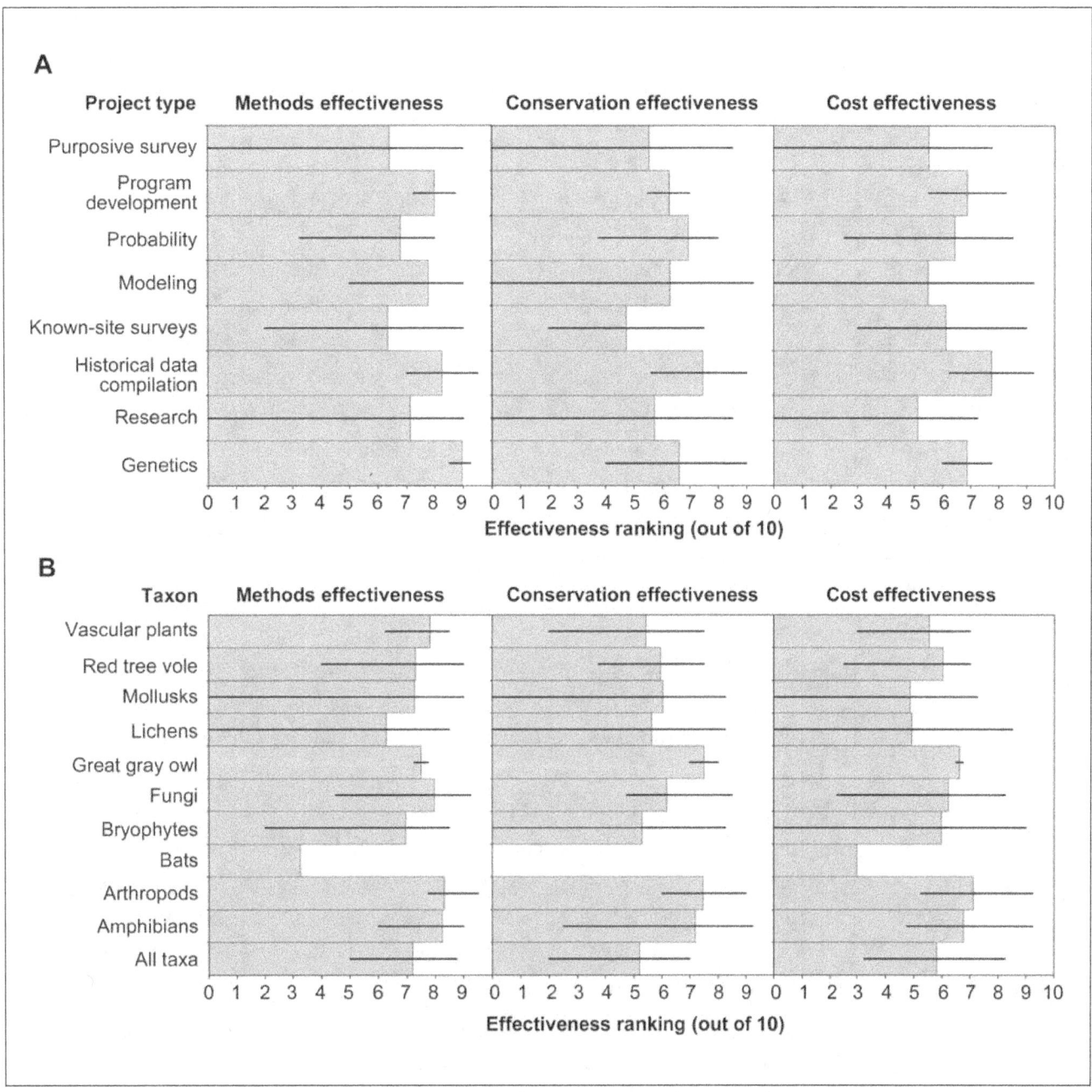

Figure 2—Panel results of effectiveness ranks (mean, range) of projects by (A) project type and (B) taxon. Methods of effectiveness addressed how well project methods were matched with its objectives. Conservation effectiveness addressed how well a project met the conservation needs of the strategic survey and survey-and-manage program. Cost effectiveness assessed conservation value of a project realtive to its direct funding from the strategic survey program.

By taxa, the two-edged sword of working with little-known species becomes apparent: effectiveness can be low owing to difficulties working with such organisms that are truly rare, but new knowledge gains can be dramatic because so little has been done with these species.

Historical data compilation projects also scored high. Both projects likely did well because these rely on straightforward techniques that directly address their very focused objectives. Purposive surveys, known-site surveys, and probability sampling had the lowest mean methods effectiveness ranks.

Historical data compilation projects (fig. 2a) had the highest mean conservation effectiveness ranks, and this result suggests that amassing prior information is a critical step in development of conservation program for a taxon. It should be noted that historical data compilations had occurred previously for several taxa, especially those assessed for the Northwest Forest Plan (e.g., Thomas et al. 1993; amphibians: biology—Blaustein et al. 1995, site locations—Olson 1999). Probability sampling projects also received high conservation effectiveness scores, suggesting this project type can be extremely valuable. By design, projects with probability sampling had inference over areas greater than the sites of the sample, and that greatly expanded their scope; for example, applications of findings to a larger geographic area would be extremely useful for conservation guidance across a region. Known-site surveys and research projects scored lowest overall for conservation effectiveness. These project types tended to answer specific site or biological questions, and had limitations owing to scope, such as lack of inference over areas greater than the sites of the surveys, relative to the other project types.

Historical data compilations, program development, and genetics had the highest cost effectiveness ranks (fig. 2a) and these results were likely due to the limited amount of field data collection and model development, both costly efforts that may be more prone to falling short of expectations. A few research projects were multiyear and multiple-partner endeavors, which may have elevated costs; these were ranked less effective when they were incomplete with a lack of accountability.

By taxa, the two-edged sword of working with little-known species becomes apparent: effectiveness can be low owing to difficulties working with such organisms that are truly rare, but new knowledge gains can be dramatic because so little has been done with these species. Lower average scores for lichens, bryophytes, mollusks, and "all taxa" reflect, in part, difficulties with executing effective project designs and yielding results advancing species conservation. Also, these were relatively lesser known taxa, such that incremental increases in site-specific knowledge of occurrence (i.e., results of purposive or known-site surveys) may not have greatly advanced their conservation. However, again, the lower scores in these categories may be just a few studies that effectively lower the group average. The great gray owl is an example of great strides in knowledge gains with direct application to species management or conservation by just two preliminary studies. It was noted that the scope of the work was narrow for these two studies, but given the lack of knowledge for the species in the Pacific Northwest as a whole, the implications of the findings were relatively dramatic. Arthropods and amphibians also ranked relatively high, perhaps because new knowledge gains were achieved owing to established and effective methods for these taxa. Unfortunately, the first attempt at conducting strategic surveys for bats via a probability sampling approach appeared to suffer from a project design and implementation issue. Similarly, design and implementation issues affected one amphibian project that used a probability sampling approach (see app. 3 for lessons learned from probability sampling).

Funding level seemed associated with project effectiveness. Many highly effective projects were funded at levels between $30,000 and 200,000. Projects funded at either greater or lesser amounts were more likely to remain incomplete. Projects funded at lower amounts also naturally tended to have limited scope. For example, several projects funded at levels <$30,000 were to search for specific species in certain locations (e.g., known-site or purposive surveys), often being opportunistic to capitalize on the juxtaposition of species experts' locations with neighboring federal lands. Although this may have been a cost-effective way to get the work done, the conservation effectiveness of such small-scale surveys may not have been great, and consequent cost effectiveness for advancing conservation may not have been great either. Some of these suffered from inadequate documentation and data management as well.

Lessons Learned

Numerous lessons were learned by our implementation and evaluation of these strategic survey projects. First, information gained from this body of work greatly advanced knowledge of species biology (app. 3, biology lessons; app. 4, products). Several projects collected data and conducted analyses to examine species-habitat associations or construct species-habitat models. Some of these were applied at landscape scales to predict species occurrences. However, only one project completed a subsequent field validation of a model applied to large spatial scales. Other projects (1) developed more refined species range boundaries; (2) documented additional habitats in which species could occur; (3) confirmed previous suspicions about habitat associations; (4) supported associations or lack of associations with LSOG conditions; (5) supported species persistence in federal reserve land allocations; (6) provided the first syntheses of data and literature for a taxon; (7) advanced survey protocols; (8) documented individual home ranges or expanded home ranges; (9) identified new species and populations; and (10) documented that species

Numerous lessons were learned by our implementation and evaluation of these strategic survey projects. First, information gained from this body of work greatly advanced knowledge of species biology.

were more common than previously known or were truly rare. Some projects illustrated the value of "mining" existing data for research questions, although these may have had limited conservation effectiveness.

Overall, species management has been advanced. Effects of thinning, patch reserves, prescribed fire, and forest edges are now known for some taxa. Also, new sites are now available for potential monitoring.

Project funding level may be important to advance species' conservation. In particular, projects funded at levels less than $30,000 were generally of small scope, lacked inference, focused on filling specific knowledge gaps, were not always completed or documented, and consequently may have resulted in limited species conservation effectiveness. The most effective projects relative to advancing species' conservation were funded at levels from $30,000 to $200,000, which may reflect costs to adequately hire personnel to design, implement, analyze, and report on full studies. Some of the more costly projects were incomplete at the time of our assessment, and may reflect more complex designs and multiple-year efforts.

Lessons were learned relative to project design and implementation. For project design, up-front planning seemed inadequate in many cases. Accountability was problematic at several levels for many projects. Inadequate oversight of projects by the strategic survey program was evident.

Lessons were learned relative to project design and implementation (app. 3, planning lessons). For project design, up-front planning seemed inadequate in many cases. Some projects were funded for single years but clearly were intended to be or quickly became multiyear endeavors. Multiyear projects may have developed owing to delayed implementation or poor planning as a result of mid-year receipt of funds, inability to implement surveys in a timely way owing to federal hiring constraints, or data collection in year one with later analyses and reporting. This likely led to the incompletion of some projects because federal funds were difficult to carry over into the following fiscal year; without funding, federal personnel may have been constrained. Design issues included narrow scope of some projects conducted in small areas or at case-study sites and lack of a random component to study designs, which could have allowed broader inference. Limited up-front planning affected several projects that ran into logistical constraints owing to access or time issues. Some projects were being conducted by agency personnel subject to shifting priorities. Project leads for some projects changed. Methods used for surveys changed in one study, mid-way through the project. Consultation with a statistician would have helped design and implementation issues for several projects. In general, project types tend to require 1 year of funding to collect data or build a model and another year to analyze the data (if necessary) or test the model. The approach of some personnel to plan and implement yearly projects toward a larger effort may be appropriate for accountability and if a change in plans is needed.

Accountability was problematic at several levels for many projects. Inadequate oversight of projects by the strategic survey program was evident by the lack of record keeping and knowledge of which projects had been funded, completed, and ongoing. Records of project proposals, objectives, and rationale for their funding were not consistently maintained. In particular, over 40 percent of projects were incomplete at the time of this evaluation, suggesting expectations from the program perspective had not been well-communicated to principal investigators. Although we asked for summary forms from principal investigators for each project, the fate of incomplete projects was uncertain, with some likely continuing and many possibly being stopped or stalled with the elimination of the survey-and-manage program in 2004. A mechanism was not evident for progress reporting, and dead-lines of projects were not developed, not being enforced, or were not enforceable. It was apparent to us in our compilation of projects that a refined process or additional personnel should have been used in the management of the many strategic survey projects. In summary, programmatic accountability seemed to consistently fall short in (1) defining expectations, (2) requiring timelines to be met, (3) requiring detailed project proposals to be submitted and maintained, (4) requiring statistically sound project designs, (5) requiring reporting, and (6) continuing to allocate monies to some people when they were not completing their work.

Ramifications of complex collaborations among investigators from multiple affiliations no doubt added to the accountability issues we detected. Retrospec-tively, we can see the need for strong program-level management to ensure two-way communication of program implementation and project accountability to bridge affiliation gaps. Formal contracts or memoranda of understanding with timelines of progress and final reports are popular mechanisms to bridge such gaps. Alter-natively, because the strategic survey program did not have direct supervision of most investigators, accountability processes could have included supervisors in the planning, implementation, and accountability of projects. Records we were able to retrieve about strategic survey projects suggested that contracts were in place when independent contractors were hired, but were used variably otherwise. For example, we could not be sure that supervisors of principal investigators within the various federal agency affiliations knew that work for strategic surveys was pro-posed, funded, in progress, a priority, and that reporting products were expected. Each affiliation and principal investigator also has their own "culture" relative to partnerships, which may have led to informal communications (telephone or email progress reports that were not recorded) or extended timelines (graduate student projects may have been multiyear to enable classes and other student obligations to be fulfilled, yet not necessarily acknowledged by the strategic survey program).

Project lead accountability also was an issue. Two projects were not conducted at all; others were not conducted as proposed; implementation of several was delayed owing to a variety of logistic or personnel issues; many were not completed; and, in some instances, data were collected but not input to the interagency species database or analyzed. Products from funded projects rarely were sent to the strategic survey program. Some projects were very long-term endeavors, yet this information was not documented as part of project planning. In one case, a single work team was funded $761,000 for a variety of projects; yet, we found only projects summing to $131,000 had apparently been completed. Again, there appeared to be lack of accountability tracking from the program and lack of accountability with implementation from the project lead sides that contributed to these issues. We recommend in such cases that at a minimum expectations should be documented at the beginning of a project and subsequent years of funding be dependent upon proven progress at meeting project objectives.

Lastly, although we found development of species-specific molecular genetic probes and habitat models to be relatively expensive endeavors, these also were noted to be highly effective to advance species conservation. These are tools relevant to most taxa groups that, given information needs, should be retained in the greater toolbox of project types for a rare species conservation program.

Opportunities

Although some of the lessons learned emphasize process improvements, we found that a great deal of new and useful data were emerging from these strategic survey projects. Organized dissemination of survey results is needed for federal resource specialists, land managers, taxa experts, and species databases. Incorporation of new species information into revised taxa syntheses, advancement of survey protocols, and management recommendations are likely future needs. Communication of project findings on agency Web sites was cited as a priority task for the agency sensitive species program for those taxa still of concern that are being managed to forestall federal listing in the region. Some project findings (e.g., collection of habitat data) could facilitate new habitat modeling efforts. A few effective studies demonstrate an approach works and could be applied to other areas or taxa. Some studies suggest new work or surveys are needed to expand the scope of findings or to address emerging themes per taxon. Our collation of science advances of completed strategic survey projects are now available in an archive at the USDA Forest Service, Pacific Northwest Region, Regional Office, Interagency Special-Status and Sensitive Species Program, Portland, Oregon. They may prove valuable for ongoing rare species management.

Our collation of science advances of completed strategic survey projects are now available in an archive at the USDA Forest Service, Pacific Northwest Region, Regional Office, Interagency Special-Status and Sensitive Species Program, Portland, Oregon. They may prove valuable for ongoing rare species management.

Summary

Strategic surveys were a successful venture for the development of more species knowledge. Many studies generated a great deal of new information regarding species distributions, habitat associations, and effects of land management activities. Results of many studies confirmed rarity or LSOG association, or determined species were more common than previously known or were associated with a broader array of habitats. In particular, these new insights have led to a greater understanding of how the federal Northwest Forest Plan land allocations and provisions may provide for biodiversity.

A toolbox of seven distinct approaches (i.e., project types) to gather species information was assembled. Application of a specific tool was appropriate under a certain set of circumstances, largely contingent upon whether a taxon was already a data-rich or data-poor entity and the geographic scope of the information need. No single project type should be advocated over all others; they all appear to have their utility under different conditions and information needs. Effectiveness of all project types was generally moderate to somewhat high, although relative differences may be useful to make decisions for future approaches relative to information need. Probability sampling offers broader geographic inference, and holds promise for greater use to answer questions related to rarity or habitat. By taxa, more projects were conducted and more funding allocated to projects with vertebrates, perhaps owing to their heightened regulatory oversight or the availability of federal agency experts.

However, administrative issues overshadowed this program of work. Given sufficient time for project completion and program adaptive management, it is possible that the problems we found in planning, implementation, and tracking projects would be resolved; the disruption of this program in 2004 may have adversely affected our findings on accountability. However, only 70 percent of projects were included in the SSIGs, suggesting the other projects may have begun without survey-and-manage oversight. Our retrospective analysis suggests the implementation process may have been deficient in various ways, insufficient personnel were assigned to manage this work, clear expectations for project leads were not defined, project leads did not always complete their work, and accountability was subsequently lost. Although it is important to reduce administrative costs so that more funding is allocated to projects for greater scientific and conservation gains, future programs are well-advised to ensure sufficient oversight and managerial tracking to achieve the results they seek. Our findings are applicable to the adaptive management of the survey-and-manage program, to the Oregon/Washington Bureau of Land Management special status

Strategic surveys were a successful venture for the development of more species knowledge. Many studies generated a great deal of new information regarding species distributions, habitat associations, and effects of land management activities. In particular, these new insights have led to a greater understanding of how the federal Northwest Forest Plan land allocations and provisions may provide for biodiversity.

species program and the Pacific Northwest Region Forest Service sensitive species programs, which are jointly administered at the regional level by the Interagency Special Status and Sensitive Species Program and which similarly funds projects to fill information gaps of species on their lists, and to other species conservation programs.

Acknowledgments

This paper is a product of the authors and although federal agency manager and policy reviews were conducted, this paper does not necessarily represent federal agency views. We greatly appreciate comments on an earlier draft from Marianne Turley, Bruce Rittenhouse, Randy Molina, and Richard Helliwell. We thank Russell Holmes for serving on the evaluation panel, Jeanne Hoxer for compiling data, and Lynne Larson for data management and analyses of Summary Forms. We especially thank Kathryn Ronnenberg for data compilation, editing, and graphic design, and Tami Lowry and Carolyn Wilson for editorial assistance.

Metric Equivalents

When you know:	Multiply by:	To find:
Acres	0.405	Hectares
Square miles	2.59	Square kilometers

Literature Cited

Blaustein, A.R.; Beatty, J.J.; Olson, D.H.; Storm, R.M. 1995. The biology of amphibians and reptiles in old-growth forests in the Pacific Northwest. Gen. Tech. Rep. PNW-GTR-337. Portland, OR: U.S. Department of Agriculture, Forest Service, Pacific Northwest Research Station. 98 p.

Forest Ecosystem Management Assessment Team [FEMAT]. 1993. Forest ecosystem management: an ecological, economic, and social assessment. Portland, OR: U.S. Department of Agriculture; U.S. Department of the Interior [and others]. [Irregular pagination].

Lindenmayer, D.B.; Franklin, J.F. 2002. Managing forest biodiversity: a comprehensive multiscaled approach. Washington, DC: Island Press. 351 p.

Meffe, G.K.; Carroll, C.R. 1997. The species in conservation. In: Meffe, G.K.; Carroll, C.R., contribs. Principles of conservation biology. 2nd ed. Sunderland, MA: Sinauer Associates, Inc.: 57–86. Chapter 3.

Miller, K.; Allegretti, M.H.; Johnson, N.; Jonsson, B. 1995. Measures for conservation of biodiversity and sustainable use of its components. In: Heywood, V.H.; Watson, R.T., eds. Global biodiversity assessment. Cambridge, United Kingdom: United Nations Environment Programme and Cambridge University Press: 915–1062. Chapter 13.

Molina, R.; Marcot, B.G.; Lesher, R. 2006. Protecting rare, old-growth forest-associated species under the survey and manage program guidelines of the Northwest Forest Plan. Conservation Biology. 20: 306–318.

Molina, R.; McKenzie, D.; Lesher, R. [and others]. 2003. Strategic survey framework for the Northwest Forest Plan survey and manage program. Gen. Tech. Rep. PNW-GTR-573. Portland, OR: U.S. Department of Agriculture, Forest Service, Pacific Northwest Research Station. 34 p.

Noss, R.F.; O'Connell, M.A.; Murphy, D.D. 1997. The science of conservation planning: habitat conservation under the Endangered Species Act. Washington, DC: Island Press. 246 p.

Olson, D.H., ed. 1999. Survey protocols for amphibians under the survey and manage provision of the Northwest Forest Plan. Version 3.0. Interagency publication of the Regional Ecosystem Office. BLM Publ. BLM/OR/WA/PT-00/033+1792. Portland, OR: U.S. Department of the Interior, Bureau of Land Management. 310 p.

Olson, D.H.; Leonard, W.P. 1997. Amphibian inventory and monitoring: a standardized approach for the Pacific Northwest. In: Olson, D.H.; Leonard, W.P.; Bury, R.B., eds. Sampling amphibians in lentic habitats. Northwest Fauna. 4: 1–21. Chapter 1.

Rittenhouse, B. 2002. 2002 strategic survey implementation guide. Version 2.4. Portland, OR: U.S. Department of the Interior, Bureau of Land Management. http://www.or.blm.gov/surveyandmanage/StrategicSurveyGuides/2002/SS_Imp_ Guide.pdf. (21 June 2006).

Rittenhouse B. 2003. 2003-2004 strategic survey implementation guide. Version 1.2. Portland, OR: U.S. Department of the Interior, Bureau of Land Management. http://www.or.blm.gov/surveyandmanage/StrategicSurveyGuides/2003/2003_ SS_Implementation_Guide.pdf. (21 June 2006).

Thomas, J.W.; Raphael, M.G.; Anthony, R.G. [and others]. 1993. Viability assessments and management considerations for species associated with late-successional and old-growth forests of the Pacific Northwest: the report of the Scientific Analysis Team. [Place of publication unknown]: U.S. Department of Agriculture. 530 p.

U.S. Department of Agriculture; U.S. Department of the Interior [USDA and USDI]. 1994a. Final supplemental environmental impact statement on management of habitat for late-successional and old-growth forest related species within the range of the northern spotted owl [Northwest Forest Plan]. Portland, OR. 2 vol.

U.S. Department of Agriculture; U.S. Department of the Interior [USDA and USDI]. 1994b. Record of decision on management of habitat for late-successional and old-growth forest related species within the range of the northern spotted owl [Northwest Forest Plan]. Portland, OR.

U.S. Department of Agriculture; U.S. Department of the Interior [USDA and USDI]. 2000. Final supplemental environmental impact statement for amendment to the survey and manage, protection buffer, and other mitigation measures standards and guidelines. Portland, OR. 2 vol.

U.S. Department of Agriculture; U.S. Department of the Interior [USDA and USDI]. 2001. Record of decision and standards and guidelines for amendments to the survey and manage, protection buffer, and other mitigation measures standards and guidelines. Portland, OR.

U.S. Department of Agriculture; U.S. Department of the Interior [USDA and USDI]. 2004a. Final supplemental environmental impact statement to remove or modify the survey and manage mitigation measure standards and guidelines. Portland, OR. 2 vol. http://www.or.blm.gov/nwfpnepa/index.htm#March 23, 2004. (30 June 2006).

U.S. Department of Agriculture; U.S. Department of the Interior [USDA and USDI]. 2004b. Record of decision to remove or modify the survey and manage mitigation measure standards and guidelines in Forest Service and Bureau of Land Management planning documents within the range of the northern spotted owl. Portland, OR. http://www.or.blm.gov/nwfpnepa/index.htm#March 23, 2004. (30 June 2006).

U.S. Department of Agriculture; U.S. Department of the Interior [USDA and USDI]. 2004c. Survey and manage: fiscal year 2003 annual status report. Portland, OR. http://www.or.blm.gov/surveyandmanage/ AnnualStatusReport/2003/S_and_M-2003.pdf. (30 August 2005).

World Commission on Forests and Sustainable Development. 1999. Our forests, our future: summary report of the world commission on forests and sustainable development. Cambridge, United Kingdom: Cambridge University Press. http://www.iisd.org/pdf/wcfsdsummary.pdf. (30 June 2006).

Appendix 1: Summary Forms Used to Compile Project Information

Summary Form
Non-Grid Strategic Surveys or Survey and Manage Projects

Please return <u>this form</u> by 8/30/04 to:

Please return <u>products</u> to:

dedeolson@fs.fed.us
Fax (541) 750-7329
Dede Olson
Pacific Northwest Research Station
3200 SW Jefferson Way
Corvallis, OR 97331

cshughes@fs.fed.us
Carol S. Hughes
USDA Forest Service, Region 6
P.O. Box 3623
333 SW First Avenue
Portland, OR 97208

Project Title:

Taxa Group(s):

Principal Investigators: (Name, affiliation, address, email, phone)

Funding Support: Direct S&M Support: Year(s) _____ Amount $_____
Indirect Support*: Yes / No Explain:

(*S&M support in other ways (e.g., salary) allowed this project to proceed, another grant, matching funds, collaboration with others, etc.)

Project Type: Purposive Surveys Known Site Surveys Modeling Research Other:

Completion Date:

Project Objective(s):

Critical Information Gaps Addressed:

Are These Gaps Named in Strategic Survey Implementation Guide? Yes / No / Don't know

Approach Used: (methods)

Data Disposition: (hard and e-copies: location, e-file name and directory)

Key Findings:

Products: (publications, abstracts, posters, reports, etc.; Please submit to Carol Hughes for S&M library)

Summary of Effectiveness to Address Knowledge Gap and Advance Species Conservation:

Appendix 2: Evaluation Form Used to Assess Project Effectiveness

Survey and Management Strategic Survey Projects
Project Evaluation Form

Project Number: _____

Project Title:_____

Is the project completed? (Yes/no):

Question	Score (1–10) or Answer (Y/N)	Average Score	Comments
Effectiveness of Project			
How effective was the project's method at addressing the objective?			
How effective was the project at addressing management and conservation needs? Information gap relevant to S&M?			
Lessons Learned			
Give a score for if the cost of the effort was worth the information gathered.			
Were there lessons learned from these methods?			
Was there an accountability problem?			
Information Sharing Priority			
Is there a need to share this information more broadly?			
If so, what is the target audience?			
How should it be shared?			
Opportunity for Additional Work			
If the work is not completed, do we need to push to get it completed?			
Has the current information been fully analyzed?			
What additional work could be done building from this project?			

Action:

Appendix 3

Lessons learned from strategic survey projects by project type (number of projects with similar comments during evaluations are indicated if >1)

Project type	Lessons learned	Type of lesson[a]
Genetics	• Genetic population structure is useful for conservation planning and adaptive management (e.g., can show two salamander species occur where one was previously recognized). Three projects.	Methods, biology
	• Molecular probes are expensive per species (e.g., fungi).	Cost
	• DNA can be extracted from old vole bones in owl pellets.	Methods, biology
Historical data compilation	• Searches of literature and previously collected data are an effective approach for initial information gathering (arthropods, lichens, bryophytes). Two projects.	Methods
	• Museums do not always reply to information requests. Site validation is difficult when historical data locations are imprecise. Historical range may differ from current distribution patterns (voles).	Methods, biology
Known-site surveys	• Small and large efforts are not always well planned or documented. Four projects (e.g., how were species chosen, how does effort link to habitat modeling, were data entered into databases, were data used in modeling efforts, etc.); study not entirely planned up front (budget, analysis, and reporting).	Planning
	• Sites surveyed are now well-poised for future monitoring efforts.	Adaptive management
	• Shifting priorities affected project completion. (If initiated, should a project be completed?Accountability needed.)	Planning
	• Species ranges were confirmed.	Biology
Modeling	• Design flaws were detected; need to have better oversight of study plans; need better documentation/reporting; modelers should communicate and work out issues better with taxa experts. Eleven projects.	Planning
	• Landscape-level analyses were effective (habitat, risk, supported lack of "rarity" for one species). Two projects.	Methods
	• Late-successional and old-growth association was supported for one species.	Biology
	• At least one project had narrow scope; it could have been designed to have more inference.	Planning, cost
	• Habitat modeling is expensive for one species.	Methods
	• Model validation was not conducted. Two projects.	Methods
	• Modeling can "mine" existing data, although conservation value of mining expeditions are not assured. Two projects.	Forest managment
	• New information emerged about landscape design; patch reserve approach seen as valid.	Planning
	• The value was questioned of a large contribution to a long-term ecology project with broad applications (potential natural vegetation model), rather than contributions to specific to rare/little-known species issues.	Planning
	• A map of all species sites was useful for implementation monitoring, to show which units were conducting predisturbance surveys.	Planning
	• A map is not a final product; need metadata and report of methods, etc.	

Project type	Lessons learned	Type of lesson[a]
Probability sampling	• Retrospective study raised questions of pretreatment conditions owing to patchy distribution of organism; collect preharvest data when possible for stronger inferences.	Planning
	• Entire project should be planned up front (methods, data collection, analysis and reporting process and standards). Six projects.	Planning
	▪ Although a report was submitted, it was not acceptable; a revised final report was not submitted. Need to clarify accountability process up front.	
	▪ Need to plan how to deal with inaccessible areas (e.g., high elevation, snowbound, roadless) that are randomly selected as part of design.	
	▪ Project expected to have a statistical design for site selection but was not implemented as such (turned into case studies rather than inferential work); analysis was needed in first year and budget should have funded entire project rather than only part of it.	
	▪ Do not modify design midway through the project and expect to draw conclusions from all data combined; was there inadequate communication between project designers and implementers—unclear why implementers changed protocol.	Planning
	• Random sampling protocol did not appear to work. Two projects.	
	▪ For one patchy salamander species, random sampling proved ineffective owing to inadequacy of remote site selection to identify suitable habitat; field crews needed to bypass areas that looked good for the species in order to sample the selected site, and some selected sites ended up not meeting criteria for sampling, which wasted time/effort (could take a day to reach a site, then find it did not meet sampling criteria).	
	▪ For coastal lichens, random sampling was not a cost-effective approach.	Biology, methods
	• An effective project looking at species occurrance in habitats in which we did not know they occurred. Two projects.	
	▪ Salamander species was found to occur in reserves, which led to a later decision to remove it from the survey-and-manage provision; however, sampling only in reserves biased the data (What is the role of matrix for this species?).	
	▪ Another salamander species was found to occur outside of rock outcrops/limestone, but does not seem to thrive there.	
Program development	• Better integration/communication is needed with taxa leads and experts. Two projects.	Planning
Purposive surveys	• Good approach of identifying gaps in species distribution where models show habitat occurs, then go and see if species is there; species found at 65 percent of sites surveyed.	Biology, methods
	• Makes sense to look outside of preconceived notion of "habitat" for rare and little-known species.	Methods
	• Good example of interagency cooperative effort.	Partners
	• More up-front planning needed. Three projects.	
	▪ Better contract administration needed; haphazard methods used and single site visit inadequate.	Planning
	▪ Shifting project leads and priorities resulted in poor implementation and uncertain data quality.	

Project type	Lessons learned	Type of lesson[a]
	• Better project documentation needed. Five projects.	
	▪ For small projects.	
	▪ Standardized survey protocol needed for opportunistic work. Two projects.	Planning
	▪ Need to document where surveys occurred and species found and not found. Three projects.	
	▪ What criteria were used for the habitat model upon which survey was based?	
Research	• Study to examine alternative survey method found method was not effective.	Method
	• Study of thinning effects and leave islands found 1-acre diameter patches retained interior microclimate and some species.	Biology, forest management
	• Case study has limited inference. Four projects.	Biology
	• Species occur to edges of intact stands, but abundances reduced near edge.	Biology, forest management
	• Funding for 1 year, but this was a multiyear project. Two projects.	Planning
	• Study found surveys for fungi should be conducted in >2 years and >300 square miles.	Methods
	• Study confirmed distribution patterns; abundance of active sites now controversial.	Planning
	• Accountability issues. Two projects.	Biology
	• Life history knowledge expanded for great gray owls, but work is intensive and has technical difficulties.	

[a] Types of lessons were categorized as methods (e.g., survey methodology), biology (new species knowledge), cost (expense of project), planning (design, implementation, documentation, reporting, or accountability issue), adaptive management (program advancement), forest management (e.g., design of forest projects or landscapes), and partners (e.g., multiple agencies).

Appendix 4

Products (N = 123) from the U.S. Pacific Northwest federal survey-and-manage program strategic survey projects and related studies on survey-and-manage species that are available at the USDA Forest Service and USDI Bureau of Land Management Interagency Special Status and Sensitive Species Program, 333 SW First Avenue, Portland, Oregon 97208. Project numbers are cross-referenced to this archive and our project summary forms and evaluations. Presentations are not included here unless abstracts were journal-published.

Project no.	Product
Amph_01, Amph_09	Mead, L.S. 2006. *Plethodon* salamanders of the Applegate, Klamath and Scott River areas: report on genetic variation and species status. Yreka, CA. February 2006 report to the U.S. Fish and Wildlife Service. 27 p. Unpublished report. On file with: D.H. Olsen, Pacific Northwest Research Station, 3200 SW Jefferson Way, Corvallis, OR 97331.
	Mead, L.S.; Clayton, D.R.; Nauman, R.S. [et al.]. 2003. Molecular and morphological variation in the *Plethodon elongatus-stormi* complex. Northwestern Naturalist. 84: 106.
	Mead, L.S.; Clayton, D.R.; Nauman, R.S. [et al.]. 2005. Newly discovered populations of salamanders from Siskiyou County California represent a species distinct from *Plethodon stormi.* Herpetologica. 61: 158–177.
Amph_02, Amph_17	Ollivier, L.M.; Welsh, H.H., Jr. 2000. A hierarchal analysis of the habitat correlates of the Siskiyou Mountains salamander (*Plethodon stormi*): as north meets south. Northwestern Naturalist. 81: 84.
	Ollivier, L.M.; Welsh, H.H., Jr.; Clayton, D.R. 2001. Habitat correlates of the Siskiyou Mountains salamander, *Plethodon stormi* (Caudata: Plethodontidae) with comments on the species' range. Arcata, CA: U.S. Department of Agriculture, Forest Service, Redwood Science Laboratory. 47 p.
	Stauffer, H.B.; Welsh, H.H., Jr. 2003. Multiscale modeling of the Siskiyou Mountains salamander (*Plethodon stormi*): exploring approaches for hypothesis generation and the development of tools for conservation planning. Northwestern Naturalist. 84: 115.
	Welsh, H.H., Jr.; Stauffer, H.B.; Clayton, D.R.; Ollivier, L.M. [2007]. Multiscale habitat relationships of the Siskiyou Mountains salamander, *Plethodon stormi,* on each side of the Siskiyou Crest. Northwest Science. 81(1): 15–36.
Amph_03	Suzuki, N.; Olson, D. 2005. Assessing threats to the conservation of Siskiyou Mountain salamanders in Oregon. In: Peterson, C.E.; Maguire, D.A., eds. Balancing ecosystem values: innovative experiments for sustainable forestry: proceedings of a conference. Gen. Tech. Rep. PNW-GTR-635. Portland, OR: U.S. Department of Agriculture, Forest Service, Pacific Northwest Research Station: 375 p.

Project no.	Product
	Suzuki, N.; Olson, D. [N.d.]. Assessment of risk to conservation of Siskiyou Mountains salamanders in the Applegate Watershed. In: Olson, D.H.; Clayton, D.R.; Reilly, E.C. [et al.]. Conservation strategy for the Siskiyou Mountains salamander (*Plethodon stormi*). Version 1.1. Portland, OR: U.S. Department of Agriculture, Forest Service, Pacific Northwest Region; U.S. Department of the Interior, Bureau of Land Management, Sensitive Species Programs: 44–49. Appendix 2.
	Suzuki, N.; Olson, D.H. 2005. Developing a GIS-based risk assessment process for the conservation of rare species across the landscape. Northwestern Naturalist. 86: 117.
	Suzuki, N.; Olson, D.H. [2007 submitted]. Biodiversity conservation in temperate planted forests of Oregon and Washington, USA. Biodiversity and Conservation.
	Suzuki, N.; Olson, D.H.; Reilly, E.C. [2006 submitted]. Developing landscape habitat models for rare amphibians with small geographic ranges: an example using Siskiyou Mountains salamanders in the western USA. Biodiversity and Conservation.
Amph_04	Nauman, R.S.; Olson, D.H. 2004. Strategic survey annual report: Siskiyou Mountains salamander northern population. Corvallis, OR: U.S. Department of Agriculture, Forest Service, Pacific Northwest Research Station. 4 p. Submitted to the Survey and Manage Program.
Amph_05	Nauman, R.S.; Lindstrand, L., III; Olson, D.H. 2003. Recent discoveries of Shasta Salamanders (*Hydromantes shastae*) in unusual habitats: relative rarity and conservation implications. Northwestern Naturalist. 84: 108.
	Nauman, R.S.; Olson, D.H. 2004. Surveys for terrestrial amphibians in Shasta County, California, with notes on the distribution of Shasta Salamanders (*Hydromantes shastae*). Northwestern Naturalist. 85: 35–38.
Amph_06	Nauman, R.S.; Olson, D.H. 2004. Distribution of the Siskiyou Mountains salamander, *Plethodon stormi,* in relation to federal land allocations in Siskiyou County, California. Northwestern Naturalist. 85: 83.
	Nauman, R.S.; Olson, D.H. 2004. Strategic survey annual report: Siskiyou Mountains salamander southern population. Corvallis, OR: U.S. Department of Agriculture, Forest Service, Pacific Northwest Research Station. 12 p. Submitted to the Survey and Manage Program.
	Nauman, R.S.; Olson, D.H. [2006 submitted]. Distribution and conservation of rare *Plethodon* salamanders on federal lands in Siskiyou County, California. Northwestern Naturalist.
Amph_07	Lindstrand, L., III. 2002. Green Mountain Shasta salamander purposive surveys. Report submitted to the Survey and Manage Program.
	New sites from these surveys are included in the map in: Lindstrand, L., III. 2000. Discovery of Shasta salamanders in atypical habitat. California Fish and Game. 86: 259-261. http://www.dfg. ca.gov/hcpb/species/t_e_spp/teamphib/shastasalamander.pdf. (5 July 2006).
	Nauman, R.S.; Olson, D.H. 2004. Surveys for terrestrial amphibians in Shasta County, California, with notes on the distribution of Shasta Salamanders (*Hydromantes shastae*). Northwestern Naturalist. 85: 35–38.

Project no.	Product
Amph_08	Mahoney, M.J. 2004. Molecular systematics and phylogeography of the *Plethodon elongatus* species group: combining phylogenetic and population genetic methods to investigate species history. Molecular Ecology. 13: 149–166.
Amph_12	Bingham, R. 2004. The phylogeography of *Hydromantes shastae.* 4 p. Unpublished report. On file with: D.H. Olson, Pacific Northwest Research Station, 3200 SW Jefferson Way, Forestry Sciences Laboratory, Corvallis, OR 97331.
	Bingham, R. and Wake, D. B. 2006. Phylogeography of *Hydromantes shastae:* implications for management. Unpublished report. On file with: D.H. Olson, Pacific Northwest Research Station, 3200 SW Jefferson Way, Corvallis, OR 97331.
Amph_13	Jones, L.L.C.; Raphael, M.G. 2000. Diel patterns of surface activity and microhabitat use by stream-dwelling amphibians in the Olympic peninsula. Northwestern Naturalist. 81: 78.
	Jones, L.L.C.; Raphael, M.G. 2001. Diel patterns of surface activity of stream from 3 ecoregions of western Washington. Northwestern Naturalist. 82: 72.
Amph_14	DeGross, D.J. 2004. Gene flow and the relationship of *Plethodon stormi* and *P. elongatus* assessed with 11 novel microsatellite loci. Corvallis, OR: Oregon State University. 52 p. M.S. thesis.
	DeGross, D.J.; Mead, L.S.; Arnold, S.J. 2003. Assessing gene flow across contact zones between *Plethodon elongatus* and *Plethodon stormi* using microsatellite markers. Northwestern Naturalist. 84: 97.
	DeGross, D.J.; Mead, L.S.; Arnold, S.J. 2004. Assessing gene flow between the closely related species, Del Norte salamander (*Plethodon elongatus*) and Siskiyou Mountains salamander (*P. stormi*), utilizing 11 novel microsatellite markers. Northwestern Naturalist. 85: 71.
	DeGross, D.J.; Mead, L.S.; Arnold, S.J. 2004. Novel tetranucleotide microsatellite markers from the Del Norte salamander (*Plethodon elongatus*) with application to its sister species the Siskiyou Mountain salamander (*P. stormi*). Molecular Ecology Notes. 4: 353–354.
Amph_15	Herman, A.E. 2003. Aspects of the ecology of the Shasta salamander, *Hydromantes shastae,* near Samwell Cave, Shasta County, California. Arcata, CA: Humboldt State University. 56 p. M.S. thesis.
	Herman, A.E.; Marks, S.B. 2002. Movement patterns and ecology of the Shasta salamander (*Hydromantes shastae*). Northwestern Naturalist. 83: 72.
	Herman, A.E.; Marks, S.B.; Welsh, H.H., Jr. 2003. Seasonal habitat use and movement patterns of the Shasta salamander (*Hydromantes shastae*). Northwestern Naturalist. 84: 101.
Amph_16	Clayton, D.; Nauman, R. 2001. The potential management implications of recent genetic and habitat research on three species of northwestern terrestrial salamanders. Northwestern Naturalist. 82: 68.
	DeGross, D.; Nauman, R.; Olson, D.H. 2001. The role of federal reserved lands for salamander persistence in southwest Oregon and northwestern California. Northwestern Naturalist. 82: 68.

Project no.	Product
	Nauman, R. 2001. Amphibian strategic survey: Del Norte/Siskiyou Mountains salamander final report. Submitted to the Survey and Manage Program.
	Nauman, R.; Olson, D. 2002. A distributional analysis of the Del Norte/Siskiyou Mountains salamander complex. Report submitted to the Survey and Manage Program.
	Nauman, R.S.; Olson, D.H. 2002. The Del Norte/Siskiyou Mountains salamander complex: status and conservation on federal lands. Northwestern Naturalist. 83: 79.
Amph_18	Henderson, J. 2004. Modeled potential habitat for Van Dyke's salamander: Southwest Washington. Maps submitted to the Survey and Manage Program.
Amph_20	Cissel, J.H.; Anderson, P.; Chan, S. [et al.]. 2004. Bureau of Land Management's density management study. Corvallis, OR: Cooperative Forest Ecosystem Research (CFER) program fact sheet. 6 p.
	Wessell, S.; Olson, D.; Schmitz, R. 2005. Preliminary research results: leave islands. Density management and riparian buffer studies research highlight. In: Erickson, J., ed. Bureau of Land Management density management studies, 2005 CFER annual report. Corvallis, OR: Cooperative Forest Ecosystem Research, Oregon State University: 40–42.
	Wessell, S.; Schmitz, R.; Olson, D. 2005. Leave islands as refugia for low-mobility species in managed forests. In: Peterson, C.E.; Maguire, D.A., eds. Balancing ecosystem values: innovative experiments for sustainable forestry: proceedings of a conference. Gen. Tech. Rep. PNW-GTR-635. Portland, OR: U.S. Department of Agriculture, Forest Service, Pacific Northwest Research Station: 379.
	Wessell, S.J. 2001. Evaluating the utility of upslope leave islands as refugia for sensitive plant and animal species in managed forests: a research proposal. Northwestern Naturalist. 82(2): 84.
	Wessell, S.J. 2005. Biodiversity in managed forests of western Oregon: species assemblages in leave islands, thinned, and unthinned forests. Corvallis, OR: Oregon State University. 161 p. M.S. thesis.
	Wessell, S.J.; Olson, D.H.; Schmitz, R.A. 2005. Effects of thinning on microclimate, plants, and low-mobility animals in managed Oregon forests. Northwestern Naturalist. 86: 122.
	Wessell, S.J.; Olson, D.H.; Schmitz, R.A. [2007 submitted]. Biodiversity in western Oregon managed forests: leave islands retain species and habitats. Forest Ecology and Mangement.
Amph_24	Lund, E.M.; Crisafulli, C.M.; McIntyre, A.P.; Turley, M. 2004. Occurrence of the Van Dyke's salamander (*Plethodon vandykei*) and other stream and seep associated amphibian species in the Washington Cascade Range. Northwestern Naturalist. 85: 81.
Amph_25	McIntyre, A.P. 2003. Ecology of populations of Van Dyke's salamanders in the Cascade Range of Washington State. Corvallis, OR: Oregon State University. 128 p. M.S. thesis.

Project no.	Product
	McIntyre, A.P.; Crisafulli, C.M.; Schmitz, R.A. 2002. Habitat associations of Van Dyke's salamanders (*Plethodon vandykei*) in the Cascade Range. Northwestern Naturalist. 83: 76.
	McIntyre, A.P.; Crisafulli, C.M.; Schmitz, R.A. 2005. Population and movement estimates of Van Dyke's salamanders (*Plethodon vandykei*) using mark-recapture techniques. Northwestern Naturalist. 86: 108.
	McIntyre, A.P.; Schmitz, R.A.; Crisafulli, C.M. 2004. Associations of the Van Dyke's salamander (*Plethodon vandykei*) with bio- physical features. Northwestern Naturalist. 85: 82.
	McIntyre, A.P.; Schmitz, R.A.; Crisafulli, C.M. 2006. Associations of the Van Dyke's salamander (*Plethodon vandykei*) with geomorphic conditions in headwall seeps of the Cascade Range, Washington State. Journal of Herpetology. 40: 309–322.
Amph_26	Trippe, L.S.; Crisafulli, C.M.; Hawkins, C.P. 2001. Development of habitat models for the Larch Mountain salamander (*Plethodon larselli*). Olympia, WA: U.S. Department of Agriculture, Forest Service, Pacific Northwest Research Station; final report; cooperative agreements PNW 98-9051-1-1A and PNW-98-9045-2-CC. 62 p. On file with: Forestry Sciences Laboratory, 3625 SW 93rd Avenue, Olympia, WA 98512-9193.
	Trippe, L.S.; Crisafulli, C.M.; Hawkins, C.P. 2003. Development of habitat-based models for the Larch Mountain salamander (*Plethodon larselli*). Northwestern Naturalist. 84: 116–117.
	Related work on the Larch Mountain salamander:
	Wagner, R.S.; Crisafulli, C.; Scott, J. [et al.]. 2002. Conservation genetics: tales of Pacific Northwest forest associated salamanders. Northwestern Naturalist. 83: 87.
	Wagner, R.S.; Haig, S.M. 2000. Phylogeographic variation, genetic structure and conservation unit designation in forest- associated terrestrial salamanders: the Oregon slender salamander and the Larch Mountain salamander. Northwestern Naturalist. 81: 90.
	Wagner, R.S.; Miller, M.P.; Crisafulli, C.M.; Haig, S.M. 2005. Geographic variation, genetic structure, and conservation unit designation in the Larch Mountain salamander (*Plethodon larselli*). Canadian Journal of Zoology. 83: 396–406.
	Wagner, S.; Haig, S.; Crisafulli, C.; Pfrender, M. 2001. Genetic tools for the management of forest-associated amphibians. Northwestern Naturalist. 82: 83.
Amph_29	Welsh, H.H., Jr.; Dunk, J.R.; Zielinski, W.J. 2006. Developing and applying habitat models using forest inventory data: an example using a terrestrial salamander. Journal of Wildlife Management. 70(3): 671–681.
Amph_32 Bryo_23	Cutler, D.R.; Edwards, T.C., Jr.; Alegria, J. [et al.]. 2003. Abundance and association analyses for the GOBIG2K mollusk and amphibian surveys with applications to Survey and Manage; final report. 94 p. Submitted to the Survey and Manage Program.
Arth_01	Niwa, C.G.; Peck, R.W. 2002. Influence of prescribed fire on carabid beetle (Carabidae) and spider (Araneae) assemblages in forest litter in southwestern Oregon. Environmental Entomology. 31: 785–796.

Project no.	Product
Arth_02	Peck, R.W.; Niwa, C.G. 2004. Longer-term effects of selective thinning on carabid beetles and spiders in the Cascade Mountains of southern Oregon. Northwest Science. 78: 267–277.
	Peck, R.W.; Niwa, C.G. 2005. Longer-term effects of selective thinning on microarthropod communities in late-successional coniferous forest. Environmental Entomology. 34: 646–655.
Arth_03	Cokendolpher, J.C.; Peck, R.W.; Niwa, C.G. 2005. Mygalomorph spiders from southwestern Oregon, USA, with descriptions of four new species. Zootaxa. 1058: 1–34.
	Halaj, J.; Peck, R.W.; Niwa, C.G. 2005. Trophic structure of a macro-arthropod litter food web in managed coniferous forest stands: a stable isotope analysis with delta ^{15}N and delta ^{13}C. Pedobiologia. 49: 109–118.
Arth_06	Brenner, G. 2001. Literature synthesis and recommendations for general surveys for forest understory and canopy gap herbivores pertinent to the southern range of the northern spotted owl; final report; submitted to the Survey and Manage Program, Portland, OR. http://www.fs.fed.us/r6/nr/fid/pubsweb/litsurvey/. (5 July 2006).
Arth_07	Moldenke, A.R.; Ver Linden, C. 2003. Literature synthesis and recommendations for general surveys for arthropods in soil, litter and coarse woody debris in the southern range of the northern spotted owl. http://www.fs.fed.us/r6/nr/fid/pubsweb/litsynth03.shtml. (5 July 2006).
Bats_01	Weller, T.J. 2006. Designing strategic survey protocols for bats; final report. 56 p. Submitted to the Survey and Manage Program.
Bats_02	Ormsbee, P.C.; Zinck, J.; Hull, R.; Scott, S. 2002. Methods for inventorying and monitoring bats using genetics. Bat Research News. 43: 4.
	Zinck, J.M.; Duffield, D.A.; Ormsbee, P.C. 2004. Primers for identification and polymorphism assessment of Vespertilionid bats in the Pacific Northwest. Molecular Ecology Notes. 4(2): 239–242.
Bryo_01	Helliwell, R. 2004. Observations and categorization of substrate for *Schistotega pennata* (Hedw.) Web. & Mohr. in the Pacific Northwest; final report. 10 p. Submitted to the Survey and Manage Program.
Bryo_04	Hastings, R.I.; Greven, H.C. 2003. *Grimmia lesherae.* In: Greven, H.C. Grimmias of the world. Leiden, The Netherlands: Backhuys Publ. 130–131. http://www.euronet.nl/users/backhuys/grgr htm. (6 July 2006).
Bryo_11	Hutten, M. 2003. *Iwatsukiella leucotricha:* proposive survey results on the Olympic Peninsula. Report submitted to the Survey and Manage Program.
Fungi_01	Molina, R.; Pilz, D.; Smith, J. [et al.]. 2001 Conservation and management of forest fungi in the Pacific Northwestern United States: an integrated ecosystem approach. In: Moore, D.; Nauta, M.M.; Evans, S.; Rotheroe, M., eds. Fungal conservation: issues and solutions. Cambridge, United Kingdom: Cambridge University Press: 19–63.
Fung_02	Castellano, M.A.; Cazares, E.; Fondrick, B.; Dreisbach, T. 2003. Handbook to additional fungal species of special concern in The Northwest Forest Plan. Gen. Tech. Rep. PNW-GTR-572. Portland, OR: U.S. Department of Agriculture, Forest Service, Pacific Northwest Research Station. 144 p.

Project no.	Product
	Castellano, M.A.; Smith, J.E.; O'Dell, T. [et al.]. 1999. Handbook to Strategy 1 fungal taxa from the Northwest Forest Plan. Gen. Tech. Rep. PNW-GTR-476. Portland, OR: U.S. Department of Agriculture, Forest Service, Pacific Northwest Research Station. 195 p.
	Cowden, M.M. 2002. A study of the current range and habitat of fuzzy sandozi conks (*Bridgeoporus nobilissimus*) throughout Pacific Northwest forests. Corvallis, OR: Oregon State University. 156 p. M.S. thesis.
	Dreisbach, T.A.; Smith, J.E.; Molina, R. 2002. Challenges of modeling fungal habitat: When and where do you find chanterelles? In: Scott, J.M.; Heglund, P.J., eds. Predicting species occurrences: issues of scale and accuracy. Covello, CA: Island Press: 475–481.
	Molina, R.; Pilz, D.; Smith, J. [et al.]. 2001. Conservation and management of forest fungi in the Pacific Northwestern United States: an integrated ecosystem approach. In: Moore D.; Nauta, M.M.; Evans, S.; Rotheroe, M., eds. Fungal conservation: issues and solutions. Cambridge, United Kingdom: Cambridge University Press: 19–63.
	Smith, J.E.; McKay, D.; Niwa, C.G. [et al.] 2004. Short-term effects of seasonal prescribed burning on the ectomycorrhizal fungal community and fine root biomass in ponderosa pine stands in the Blue Mountains of Oregon. Canadian Journal of Forest Research. 34: 2477–2491.
	Smith, J.E.; Molina, R.; Huso, M. [et al.]. 2002. Species richness, abundance, and composition of hypogeous and epigeous ectomycorrhizal fungal sporocarps in young, rotation-age, and old-growth stands of Douglas-fir (*Pseudotsuga menziesii*) in the Cascade Range of Oregon, U.S.A. Canadian Journal of Botany. 80: 186–204.
Fung_03	Cowden, M.M. 2002. A study of the current range and habitat of fuzzy sandozi conks (*Bridgeoporus nobilissimus*) throughout Pacific Northwest forests. Corvallis, OR: Oregon State University. 156 p. M.S. thesis.
Fung_04	Dunham, S.M.; Kretzer, A.; Pfrender, M.E. 2003. Characterization of Pacific golden chanterelle (*Cantharellus formosus*) genet size using co-dominant microsatellite markers. Molecular Ecology. 12: 1607–1618.
	Dunham, S.M.; O'Dell, T.E.; Molina, R. 2003. Analysis of nrDNA sequences and microsatellite allele frequencies reveals a cryptic chanterelle species *Cantharellus cascadensis* sp. nov. from the American Pacific Northwest. Mycological Research. 107: 1163–1177.
	Kretzer, A.M.; Dunham, S.; Molina, R.; Spatafora, J.W. 2003. Microsatellite markers reveal below ground clone structure in two species of *Rhizopogon* forming tuberculate ectomycorrhizae on Douglas-fir. New Phytologist. 161: 313–320.
	Kretzer, A.M.; Luoma, D.L.; Molina, R.; Spatafora, J. 2003. Taxonomy of the *Rhizopogon vinicolor* species complex based on analysis of ITS sequences and microsatellite loci. Mycologia. 95: 480–487.
Fung_05	Gordon, M. 2004. The development and testing of specific DNA probes for *Albatrellus ellisii* and *Albatrellus flettii*. Reports I, II, and III. Submitted to the Survey and Manage Program.
Fung_10, Fung_18	Norvell, L.L.; Exeter, R.L. 2002. The epigeous ectomycorrhizal basidiomycete Douglas-fir fungal community in "peace" and "war." Inoculum. 53(3): 47.

Project no.	Product
	Norvell, L.L.; Exeter, R.L. 2002. 547—The Douglas-fir epigeous ecto-mycorrhizal basidiomycete community in the western North American northern spotted owl zone. In: The 7th international mycological congress—IMC7: Book of abstracts. Olso, Norway: 166–167. http://www.uio.no/conferences/imc7. (5 July 2006).
	Norvell, L.L.; Exeter, R.L. 2004. Ectomycorrhizal epigeous basidio-mycete diversity in Oregon Coast Range *Pseudotsuga menziesii* forest—preliminary observations. In: Cripps, C.L., ed. Fungi in forest ecosystems: systematics, diversity and ecology. New York: The New York Botanical Garden: 159–189.
	Norvell, L.L.; Redhead, S.A. 2000. *Stropharia albivelata* and its basionym *Pholiota albivelata*. Mycotaxon. 76: 315–320.
Lich_01	Carlberg, T.; Carothers, S.; Hoover, L. 2004. Spatial modeling for *Usnea longissima, Ramalina thrausta,* and *Lobaria oregana* in Northern California: an approach based on existing sites. Report submitted to the Survey and Manage Program.
Lich_06	Henderson, J.A.; Lesher, R.D. 2002. Survey protocols for habitat model validation for survey and manage bryophytes, lichens, vascular plants and fungi. Report submitted to the Surevey and Manage Program.
	Lesher, R.D. 2005. An environmental gradient model predicts the spatial distribution of potential habitat for *Hypogymnia duplicata* in the Cascade Mountains of northwestern Washington. Seattle, WA: University of Washington. 85 p. Ph.D. dissertation.
Lich_11, Lich_16 Lich_17	Glavich, D.A.; Geiser, L.H. 2004. *Dermatocarpon meiophyllizum* in the Pacific Northwest. Evansia. 21(3): 137–140.
	Geiser, L.H.; Glavich, D.A.; Mikulin, A.G. [et al.]. 2004. New records of rare and unusual coastal lichens from the US Pacific Northwest. Evansia. 21(3): 104–110.
	Glavich, D.A.; Geiser, L.H.; Mikulin, A.G. 2005a. Distribution of some rare coastal lichens in the Pacific Northwest and their association with late-seral and federally protected forests. The Bryologist. 108(2): 241–254.
	Glavich, D.A.; Geiser, L.H.; Mikulin, A.G. 2005b. Rare epiphytic coastal lichen habitats, modeling, and management in the Pacific Northwest. The Bryologist. 108(3): 377–390.
Lich_18	Edwards, T.C., Jr.; Cutler, D.R.; Geiser, L. [et al.]. 2004. Assessing rarity of species with low detectability lichens in Pacific Northwest forests. Ecological Applications. 14(2): 414–424.
Moll_13	Wilke, T.; Duncan, N. 2004. Phylogeographical patterns in the American Pacific Northwest: lessons from the arionid slug *Prophysaon coeruleum.* Molecular Ecology. 13(8): 2303–2315.
Moll_14	Lindberg, D.R.; Cordero, A. 2002. Molecular phylogeny of some land snails of the Clades Monadenia and Helminthoglypta in Southern Oregon and Northern California. Report to Roseburg BLM, purchase order HRP000506.
	(information used in) Roth, B.; Sadeghian, P.S. 2003. Checklist of the land snails and slugs of California. Contributions in Science 3. Santa Barbara, CA: Santa Barbara Museum of Natural History. 69 p.

Project no.	Product
Moll_15	McGraw, R.; Duncan, N.; Cazares, E. 2002. Fungi and other items consumed by the blue-gray taildropper slug (*Prophysaon coeruleum*) and the papillose taildropper slug (*Prophysaon dubium*). The Veliger. Berkeley, CA: California Malacozoological Society, Inc. 45(3): 261–264.
Moll_16	Duncan, N. 2005. Monitoring of known mollusk sites following a wildfire event in 2002. Report submitted to the Survey and Manage Program.
	Hohenlohe, P.A.; Duncan, N. 2003. How do terrestrial mollusk populations survive fire? Northwestern Naturalist. 84: 102.
Moll_18	Wilke, T. 2001. Phylogeny, taxonomy, and population structure of *Hemphillia burringtoni* and *H. glandulosa* based on genetic and morphological analyses: a study plan. 8 p. Report submitted to the Olympic National Forest.
Moll_21	Dunk, J.R.; Zielinski, W.J.; Preisler, H.K. 2004. Predicting the occurrence of rare mollusks in northern California forests. Ecological Applications. 14(3): 713–729.
Moll_22	Dunk, J.R.; Zielinski, W.J.; Welsh, H.H. 2006. Evaluating reserves for species richness and representation in northern California. Diversity and Distributions. 12: 434–442.
	Dunk, J.R.; Zielinski, W.J.; West, K. [et al.]. 2002. Distributions of rare mollusks relative to reserved lands in northern California. Northwest Science. 76: 249–256.
Other_01	Boughton, D. 2001. Paradoxes in science: a new view of rarity. Science Findings 35. Portland, OR: U.S. Department of Agriculture, Forest Service, Pacific Northwest Research Station. 5 p.
	Boughton, D.; Malvadkar, U. 2002. Extinction risk in successional landscapes subject to catastrophic disturbances. Conservation Ecology. 6(2): 2. http://www.consecol.org/vol6/iss2/art2/. (5 July 2006).
	Earlier relevant work, not funded by Survey and Manage:
	Boughton, D.A.; Smith, E.R.; O'Neill, R.V. 1999. Regional vulnerability: a conceptual framework. Ecosystem Health. 5(4): 312–322.
Other_02	Molina, R.; Marcot, B.G.; Lesher, R. [2006]. Protecting rare, old-growth, forest-associated species under the Survey and Manage Program guidelines of the Northwest Forest Plan. Conservation Biology. 20(2): 306–318.
	Molina, R.; McKenzie, D.; Lesher, R. [et al.]. 2003. Strategic survey framework for Northwest Forest Plan Survey and Manage Program. Gen Tech. Rep. PNW-GTR-573. Portland, OR: U.S. Department of Agriculture, Forest Service, Pacific Northwest Research Station. 34 p.
Other_08	Morey, S.; Collins, M. 2003. Uncovering biodiversity in the Northwest Forest Plan. Northwestern Naturalist. 84: 108.
RTV_03, RTV_05, RTV_06	Bellinger, M.R.; Haig, S.M.; Forsman, E.D.; Mullins, T.D. 2005. Taxonomic relationships among *Phenacomys* voles as inferred by cytochrome b. Journal of Mammalogy. 86(1): 201–210.
	Haig, S.; Mullins, T.; Forsman, E.D. 2001. Taxonomic identity, population structure, and status in the red tree vole. Northwest Forest Plan Research Update: FY2001. 4 p. Unpublished report.

Project no.	Product
	Miller, M.P.; Bellinger, M.R.; Forsman, E.D.; Haig, S.M. 2006. Effects of historical climate change, habitat connectivity, and vicariance on genetic structure and diversity across the range of the red tree vole (*Phenacomys longicaudus*) in the Pacific North- western United States. Molecular Ecology. 15: 145–159.
RTV_04	Forsman, E.D.; Anthony, R.G.; Meslow, E.C.; Zabel, C.J. 2004. Diets and foraging behavior of northern spotted owls in Oregon. Journal of Raptor Research. 38: 214–230.
	Forsman, E.D.; Anthony, R.G.; Zabel, C.J. 2004. Distribution and abundance of red tree voles in Oregon based on occurrence in pellets of northern spotted owls. Northwest Science. 78(4): 294–302.
RTV_08	Swingle, J.K. 2005. Daily activity patterns, survival and movements of red tree voles (*Arborimus longicaudus*) in Western Oregon. Corvallis, OR: Oregon State University. 121 p. M.S. thesis.
	Swingle, J.K.; Forsman, E.D.; Sovern, S.G. 2004. A method for live-trapping tree voles. Northwestern Naturalist. 35: 134–135.
RTV_11, RTV_15	Biswell, B.L.; Jones, J.M.; Finley, L.; Schmalenberger, F. 2004. Red tree vole strategic survey results for the 2000 Klamath RTV study in Siskiyou County, California. 53 p. Report submitted to the Survey and Manage Program.